```
RMC      Klein, Shmuel Yaakov
371      To teach a Jew
KLE

15286
```

To Teach a Jew

To Teach a Jew

RATNER MEDIA AND TECHNOLOGY CENTER
JEWISH EDUCATION CENTER OF CLEVELAND

Rabbi Shmuel Yaakov Klein

Targum/Feldheim

First published 2001
Copyright © 2001 by Shmuel Yaakov Klein
ISBN 1-56871-277-4

All rights reserved

No part of this publication may be translated, reproduced, stored in a retrieval system, or transmitted in any form or by any means, electronic, mechanical, photocopying, recording, or otherwise, without prior permission in writing from both the copyright holder and the publisher.

Published by:
Targum Press, Inc.
22700 W. Eleven Mile Rd.
Southfield, MI 48034
E-mail: targum@netvision.net.il
Fax toll free: (888) 298-9992

Distributed by:
Feldheim Publishers
200 Airport Executive Park
Nanuet, NY 10954
www.feldheim.com

Printed in Israel

מכתב ברכה
הגאון הרב דב שורצמן שליט"א
ראש הישיבה, ישיבת בית התלמוד עיה"ק ירושלים

בס"ד
אלול תשמ"ה

כבוד ידיד הר"ר שמואל קליין שליט"א

עיינתי בכמה מקומות בספרו ומצאתי בו דברים מועילים, ורואים את המחנך שמרגיש הדברים שהוא כותב ושהם דברים היוצאים מן הלב, ובודאי יהיו הדברים לתועלת לרבים וישפיעו על הרבה מאחינו בנ"י לראות את האור הנמצא בתורתנו הק' ויאירו הדברים באור האמת לבבות מבנ"י בידידות רבה. ובברכת כתיבה וחתימה טובה,

דב שורצמן

Contents

Preface 9

Part One: HOW DID WE GET HERE?
   Introduction 15
   The First Yeshivah 17

Part Two: THE CHALLENGES
   Introduction 29
   Troubling Statistics 31
   So What Are You in Now? 37
   Financial Plight 40
   The Problem of Being Exact 44

Part Three: ORIENTATION
   Introduction 53
   It's Not Just Curriculum! 54
   Equitability and Nepotism 60
   Middos and Derech Eretz 63
   Cross-fire 1 74
   Ethics for the Teacher 83

Part Four: GIRLS' EDUCATION
    Introduction 115
    Chazal and Halachah. 117
    The Contemporary Movement. 130
    Chinuch HaBanos: A Qualitative Definition . 135

Part Five: GENERAL STUDIES IN THE YESHIVAH
    Introduction 145
    Kodesh versus Chol. 148
    Does Chol Belong in the Yeshivah? 160
    Who Will Teach Our Children Chol? 165

Part Six: SPECIAL STUDENTS
    Introduction 173
    Labels 178

Part Seven: VARIED VIEWPOINTS
    Introduction 185
    The Great Divide 187
    Through the Cracks 189
    Cross-fire 2 196

    Postscript 205

Preface

Nearly a quarter of a century has gone by since I first stepped into a classroom as a full-time teacher. It was a class of girls, and I was teaching *limudei kodesh*. I have been in the magical world of *chinuch* ever since.

It was a choice I made, and I wish I could say with all honesty that it was a choice that never gave me any regrets. But I cannot. Nothing in life is all of anything; it is always a bit of this and a bit of that. So it is with my chosen vocation. If you were to ask me, "What has predominated for you as a *mechanech* — the bad moments or the good ones?" I would answer flippantly, "I haven't been counting." Yet in truth, while I feel that few things in the world can compare with the frustrations of *chinuch*, even fewer can compete with it for its sense of fulfillment.

One thing integral to my particular view on the matter is that I have known numerous and multifaceted *chinuch* venues. They include (not in order of preference) teaching *kodesh* to junior-high girls, teaching *kodesh* to high-school boys, teaching *chol* to junior-high girls, teaching *chol* to high-school boys, teaching *ba'alei teshuvah*, teaching *ba'alos teshuvah*, being a principal of *chol* in a chassidic cheder, being an assistant principal of *limudei kodesh* in a girls' school, being a principal of *chol* in a *litvishe* cheder, teaching in an afternoon congregational-type school, teaching young married men just out of *kollel*, teaching a varied-background group of men from the Jewish community, and lecturing extensively in various outreach programs. I think that has exhausted the list, but you get the picture. I have experienced much of what can be experienced in *chinuch*. Although there are differences, there is sufficient shared ground among these roles for me to present the common issues.

On that basis I want to share some of what I have discovered. Some of the lighter moments as well as some of the more effective approaches I've used. Some of the proper Torah *hashkafos* on Jewish education and some of the varied experiences. Some of the doubts, some of the frustrations, and the exhilaration and reward that come only from this field.

Though I seek to share these points of view primarily with the lay community, I speak also to prospective *mechanchim* and *mechanchos* who are about to get their feet wet in this illustrious world. The layman will undoubtedly benefit from learning about the challenges their children's teachers face, the skills they will need to master, and the responsibilities they will need to assume. (Besides, in so many respects the techniques of parenting are merely modified applications of the techniques of teaching.) At the same time, a new *mechanech* can derive fortification — and perhaps even some excitement — from these pages.

I wish to express my *tefillah* to the *Ribbono shel Olam* that nothing negative come about from *To Teach a Jew* and that the *hashkafos* found here conform with *da'as Torah*, which is the single criterion of kashrus that a Jew ought to seek.

I wish to acknowledge the editors and staff of Targum Press for their valuable assistance in preparing this work for preparation. My gratitude also to Rabbi Meir Uri Gottesman, a friend and colleague, who established the connection between myself and the people at Targum. My unending gratitude to all the members of my family, whose patience was a key component in enabling me to devote myself to this project. And to the many hundreds of *talmidim* and *talmidos*, whose lives have overlapped with mine over nearly three decades and who have provided me with a bit of wisdom that only experience can furnish, my blessings and thanks.

And finally, I wish to dedicate this work to my life's partner, who has shared with me, in addition to everything else, the *igra rama*, as well as the *bira amikta*, of being in *chinuch*.

Kislev 5761

Part One

HOW DID WE GET HERE?

Introduction

It strikes me that it makes sense in exploring the topic of education to first examine the origins of Jewish education.

Formal schooling is something we all take for granted. In every state — with the exception of some Third World countries — there are schools for young people. And although the pedagogic regulations and curricula may vary from place to place, the universality of schooling is unquestioned.

It is curious to note, however, that universal — or public — education is a relatively new feature of Western society. It was only in the middle of the nineteenth century, for instance, that compulsory education was introduced in North America. Prior to that there may have been schools, but they were the luxury of the privileged class. Even in the Middle Ages and the Renaissance, there were schools for the rich and noble classes of Europe, but they taught only a tiny fraction of the overall population. During the Industrial Revolution, children were operating the machinery of mass production in sweatshops and factories, not developing their minds and their horizons.

So while today, in nearly every democratic country, there are laws against child labor and laws protecting the rights of all individuals to receive an education provided by society, this is not the way things have always been.

With respect to *klal Yisrael*, however, education for all children has been a way of life. State- or community-sponsored education is not a recent innovation within Jewish society. And, even more profound, the fundamental nature of Torah *chinuch* is in sharp contradistinction to that of general education.

In truth, there are numerous differences, but these are just the symptoms rather than the cause. If we look into the birth and charter of Jewish education, we will come to see the uniqueness — and the sanctity — of *chinuch*.

The First Yeshivah

Originally *chinuch* was the exclusive realm of parents. This, in fact, is recommended as an ideal in the Torah: "And *you* shall teach them [the words of the Torah] to *your sons*" (*Devarim* 11:19). Teaching one's son is one of the obligations listed by Chazal that a father has regarding his son, along with bris milah and teaching one's son a livelihood (Mishnah, *Kiddushin* 29a). A father's responsibility to teach his son Torah is second only to his obligation to learn Torah himself. The Torah implies this clearly by the close juxtaposition of those two concepts (*Devarim* 6:6–7).

The accepted opinion of Rabbi Yehudah (*Kiddushin* 29a) is that if a man must choose between learning Torah himself and paying for his son to learn, he himself takes priority, but only in the event that his son is not more sharp-witted and capable than he is. Otherwise the son comes first. So closely linked are the learning of the father and that of the son.

Yet in our own day, and for many centuries past, the task of educating the young Jew has been transferred to the *melamed*. We might be tempted, then, to infer that Jewish fathers have been shirking their responsibility all those years. In a certain sense this is so.

We mentioned that bris milah is among the father's obligations regarding his son. There again, in the vast majority of cases, the father does not perform the circumcision himself, but rather delegates the task to a *mohel*. Our *poskim* have explained, however, that the *mohel* performs the service on behalf of the father, acting as a *shaliach*, an extension of the father's powers. Thus, though the mitzvah is physically performed by someone else, credit for it is given to the father, since he has appointed the *mohel* to act on his behalf. Similarly, the *melamed* teaches on behalf of the father, acting as a *shaliach*. The father, by arranging for the *shaliach* to teach his son, is accredited for the *chinuch* of the child, even though the teacher is the one actually performing this duty.

So how is the father shirking his responsibility? Although Chazal have declared numerous times that "*shlucho shel adam kemoso*," that the actions a person's agent does on his behalf (apart from sins) are attributed to the person, the Gemara (*Kiddushin* 41a) nevertheless points out that it is preferable for a person to perform a righteous act by himself rather than give it to a *shaliach* to perform. Rashi articulates that there is greater merit in a person's active involvement in a commandment than in another's involvement on his behalf. It becomes more personal and has more impact. Here is where we might find the shirking of responsibility. Insofar as almost all of *chinuch* is carried out by teachers, the involvement of fathers in the mitzvah is somewhat less than it should be.

My intention is not to place blame on the shoulders of Jewish fathers. After all, there is ample reason for this situation. My goal is merely to place the Jewish school in proper perspective. Its purpose is to act on behalf of Jewish fathers. The school, therefore, is the *shaliach* of the parents in fulfilling a duty which, for various reasons, the fathers themselves do not fulfill.

LET US LOOK at the historical roots of this phenomenon. The very first thing to consider is that universal schooling for young Jewish boys was esbalished more than two millennia ago (if you are wondering about Jewish girls, take a look at part 4). It seems little wonder that we are referred to as the "people of the Book"; after all, we have had an academic orientation throughout our history.

The actual source of Jewish schooling is to be found in the monumental efforts of a giant of compassion, piety, foresight, and social sensitivity. His name was Yehoshua ben Gamla, a *kohen gadol* who served in the second Beis HaMikdash during the reign of King Alexander Yannai (103–76 B.C.E.). The Gemara relates to us the accomplishment of Yehoshua ben Gamla in the field of *chinuch*, along with the rationale underlying his initiatives:

> In the beginning, he who had a father, his father would teach him Torah; he who had no father would learn no Torah. Later they instituted that teachers would teach in Yerushalayim. Still, he who

had a father, his father would bring him up [to Yerushalayim] and [the teacher] would teach him; he who had no father would not come up and learn. So they instituted that there should be teachers in every region, and they would bring in the students when they would be sixteen or seventeen years of age. He whose teacher would be angry with him would rebel and leave. Then came Yehoshua ben Gamla, who instituted that there should be teachers in every state and in every city, and they would bring in the students when they were six or seven years of age.*

(Baba Basra 21a)

"In the beginning" — prior to the era of Yehoshua ben Gamla — there were no Jewish schools. Each father instructed his own son in the words and ways of Torah. Clearly, in an earlier part of our history, Jewish fathers seemed to have fulfilled their educational role completely.

Why, then, the need for schools? The need arose out of a concern for the orphans, who were unable to learn Torah because of a lack of the only available type of rebbe at the time. Due to this there was a series of experiments with the schooling concept, which culminated in the days of Yehoshua ben Gamla, with his enterprising en-

---

* According to *Tosafos*, the age when the child began formal studies — whether at six or seven — would be determined by his strength and personal character. According to Rabbeinu Asher, the student would start school at age six, but his father was expected to prepare him at age five.

deavors. So what proved to be a crucial feature of our nation began with a concern for a small minority, the orphans of *klal Yisrael*.

The fact that Yehoshua ben Gamla's attainment was so profound is attested to by a remark made by Rabbi Yehudah in the name of Rav just before the *gemara* cited above: "If it were not for him [Yehoshua ben Gamla], the Torah would have been forgotten by Israel." Ben Gamla was not responsible only for the introduction of community schools; he actually preserved Torah itself. Since Torah is the very lifeblood of our people, it can be said that he saved the entire *klal Yisrael* from irrevocable perdition.

The achievement is known, then. What remains to be clarified is two issues. First, why was his accomplishment so remarkable that it was considered the salvation of our nation? Second, what was the nature of his accomplishment? In which essential ways did he effect a change in the situation?

WHY WAS YEHOSHUA ben Gamla remarkable? Why would Torah have been forgotten without him? After all, the fathers of the people *were* learning Torah with their sons. And although under those circumstances the orphans would have had no opportunity to study Torah, surely such cases comprised only a tiny segment of the people. The majority of Israel were pursuing Torah despite the unfortunate plight of the orphans. Why, then, is Yehoshua ben Gamla given credit for securing the future of our Torah?

There are two approaches to answer this question.

They revolve around two primary foundations of *chinuch*: foresight and compassion.

As long as the people of Israel were leading a mostly agrarian existence, peacefully, on the soil of their forefathers, as long as they maintained a relative degree of security and self-determination, it was possible for the education of the young to be carried out in the manner of the pre–Ben Gamla days described by the Gemara. Fathers were farmers, artisans, or local merchants; their greatest worldly concerns revolved around family and social life. Fathers had both the time and the peace of mind to spend time each day with their sons studying and teaching Torah.

Well before Yehoshua ben Gamla entered the scene, however, the Jews had already experienced significant upheaval — the *galus* in Babylon, the rule of the Persian Empire, the Greek conquest, the Hasmonean revolt, to name a few. Jewish consciousness had been jolted for all time. The new Jewish mind would struggle with anxiety and with the need to worry about upcoming turbulence, even catastrophe. They were, however, still complacent enough to keep their eyes closed to the future.

Then along came the hero of Jewish education. Perhaps he foresaw the Roman conquest and the inevitable restrictions that would be decreed by Roman rule. Perhaps he foresaw the destruction of the second Beis HaMikdash. Perhaps he even prophesied the impending *galus* and its devastating proportions. We have no written legacy of any prophecy, so we cannot be certain about what he did in fact forecast. However, we can reasonably suggest that the man was overcome by a sense of foreboding from the great trials he knew his people would have to endure. He turned his fears into action, doing what he could to safeguard the spiritual future.

His suspicions materialized. Being torn away from the land of his heritage, cornered into restrictive and often shameful occupations, the Jewish father lost the time he needed to devote himself to his children's education. Persecuted, oppressed, massacred, and banished, Jewish fathers found themselves without the composure necessary for adequately teaching their children. The sweep of centuries would render a scenario drastically different from the idyllic pre–Ben Gamla one described.

It was this kind of scenario, perhaps, that Yehoshua ben Gamla conjured up in his mind. He realized that a time would come when *all* Jewish children would be orphans, in the sense that they would not have fathers who were properly predisposed to teaching them. So he made provisions for the future. Schools would replace the beleaguered fathers and teach the sons even from a very young age. We would become a nation of spiritual orphans. What was at one point a small minority would become a majority.

Thus, Rabbi Yehudah did not exaggerate when he accredited Yehoshua ben Gamla — a pillar of foresight — with the salvation of *klal Yisrael*.

THE SECOND APPROACH follows more mystical lines. The Mishnah proclaims: "Upon three things the world stands: Torah, service of the Almighty, and acts of *chessed* [lovingkindness]" (*Avos* 1:3). Consider any object that stands upon three supports, such as a stool. If one of the three supports falls, the structure is imperiled. None of the supports is expendable.

The well-being of the Jewish people — of the whole universe — relies on the continued existence of all three elements, Torah, *avodah*, and *chessed*. There is certainly Torah and divine worship in the world, but man is wont to feel indifferent toward his fellow man. According to numerous later prophets, the eventual dismantling of the northern monarchy of Yisrael would be effected primarily due to *chamas*, crimes against man and corruption, rather than as a result of any other category of sin.

In addition, if the entire universe is dependent on these three things, then logically the three supports are dependent on one another as well. Without *chessed*, there can hardly be Torah.

Yehoshua ben Gamla was confronted by a situation in which he felt there were at best two of the three pillars sustaining the world. The Beis HaMikdash stood. In it, despite the numerous deficiencies that circumscribed the second Beis HaMikdash, the prescribed *avodah* was more or less being carried out. There was Torah study, as even the Gemara points out: those who had fathers were learning with them, or because of them. The orphans, however, were being neglected.

A cardinal crime — apathy toward the plight of the unfortunate — was being committed. Moreover, as Ben Gamla saw it, the very pursuit of Torah itself seemed to be resting on this foundation of apathy. The *chinuch* of Ben Gamla's day seemed to him to be lacking compassion. He thus invested his efforts in infusing this missing trait into *chinuch*. The result was a school where *every* child could come and learn, regardless of his being blessed with any particular benefit in life, even a father. His accomplishment, then, was a display of human compassion.*

Yehoshua ben Gamla, as the father of the Jewish school, must also have been the archetypal *mechanech*, since a father begets progeny in his own image. Therefore no attempt at Torah education can be considered to be founded in the spirit of Torah unless it adheres to the basic principles that motivated Yehoshua ben Gamla — foresight and compassion.

It is clear that parents, in the way they interact with their children, act with almost unbridled compassion. They also aspire to having foresight so as to know what is best for their children. As the *shelichim* of parents, educators are usually expected to adopt these points of view as much as is feasible.

A *mechanech* is advised to assimilate these ideas in his heart as soon as he sets foot into the classroom and allow it to be manifest in every aspect of his dealings with the "anointed ones" of the Almighty.

---

* The Maharal wrote (*Nesiv HaTorah*, ch. 10) in a similar vein that in his day, the late sixteenth century, the wealthy cared only about the education of their own children and paid no attention to the needs of the children of the poor. He wrote that this caused the tremendous perdition of Torah in his time. And although this thought is more a statement of the fact that Torah will emanate primarily from "the sons of the poor," as *Chazal* say, it is possible to add our reasoning to the predicament he described so dramatically.

Part Two

THE CHALLENGES

Introduction

I have come to notice that the world appears to be divided into two distinct groups: those who are in *chinuch* and those who are not. And although the two groups overlap in many ways, in effect the twain shall never meet. That is how different and often contradictory their perspectives are.

In the great tomes of philosophy, an issue known as "the problem of other minds" is grappled with. The debate surrounds the description of barriers to communication, which obstruct one's true understanding of other people, their perceptions, and their experiences. These barriers are created by the simple fact that no one can perceive the world through another person's subjective state of mind. Thus it can hardly be expected that someone who is not in *chinuch* can fully understand someone who is. (The reverse stands a far greater chance, though, due to the fact that most *mechanchim* are also parents.)

Still, when one at least makes the attempt to describe his subjective view, he helps to bridge the gap to some extent. This, then, is an important task in *chinuch* and one that has been all but neglected. The *mechanech's* worldview must be known to the parents of their young charges. Based on the sound assumption that parents have the desire to work harmoniously and in tandem with their children's *mechanchim*, parents would benefit from learning what challenges today's Jewish educators face.

(One more thing: the problem of other minds also prevents me from claiming that I can speak on behalf of all *mechanchim*. Still, I am reasonably sure I speak for most.)

Troubling Statistics

I remember reading a few years ago, in some psychology magazine, an article that included statistics about such things as burnout and suicide in various vocational fields. What I learned was most shocking, especially in light of the fact that over a decade had passed since I made *chinuch* my own vocational choice.

What I expected to find, as my eager eyes glossed over the lines of the well-researched piece, was that it had to be people such as garment-industry or automobile-assembly workers who fared the worst, ostensibly because of the drudgery of their jobs. In anticipation of that discovery I paused and tried to imagine what it must feel like to make the same monotonous motions with the same boring tools hour after hour, day after day. How maddening, I concluded.

What ended up being maddening, much to my chagrin, was that workers who spend the better parts of their waking lives on an assembly line appeared to actually fare quite a bit better than…yes, than educators. Seven years was the number cited as the average term of service that will elapse before our most illustrious pedagogues turn sour on their work and become, to use the vernacular, burned out.

I was particularly horrified at the time. I contemplated that since more than ten years had passed since I myself had entered the perilous field, either I must be burned out without realizing it or I must have above-average stamina. Or else I was too burned out to feel even that.

Even as I was grappling with the psychological ramifications of that first bit of statistical fact, I was treated to a second blow. It appears that educators enjoyed the quite respectable second place in the suicide playoffs, second only to doctors.

For a second I felt rather honored to be grouped alongside the venerable physician. Then the terrifying implications began to sink in. Education is obviously a very rough and tumble field, fraught with intense stress and anxiety, not very different from the tremendous pressures associated with medicine. I instantly recalled that old adage: any person who wants to go into psychiatry ought to have his head examined. I wondered if it might not be true that a person who is contemplating a life as an educator might not be better off getting some more schooling.

In the special world of *chinuch*, Jewish education, it was common to hear the occasional wizened veteran of the trade share a famous quip often attributed to Rav Shimon Shkop, *zt"l*. Apparently he was wont to say that there are two things he could not expect to see surviving to a ripe old age: the horse and the *melamed*. In both cases the longevity would be indications that he (or it) had not been working to capacity. How heartening to hear that my calling might entail a preclusion of survival.

As a matter of fact, I often pause to consider how many elderly gentlemen are engaged in *chinuch*. It is mostly energetic younger men, rising to the distant call of a mission. But what happens to them after a while? Of course, we could hardly do justice to that question, because it ends up being an individual choice. One thing is evident, however: there are just not a great many *melamdim* with white beards. Somewhere along the line most fall to the wayside, casualties in the relentless battles of self-fulfillment and fiscal viability. But as time goes by, I become more and more haunted by the lament, "Where have all the *melamdim* gone?"

THE FIELD OBVIOUSLY does not hold the greatest attraction to those who contemplate entering it. I thought it might be worthwhile to consider why this is so.

When I was much younger and thinking about the various options that lay before me, I considered *chinuch* as a viable choice. I went to consult with a rebbe of mine, a *gadol* who was one of North America's most illustrious contemporary *roshei yeshivah*. "Rebbe," I said to him, "I'm thinking about what I should do after *kollel*, and one of the things I am considering is *chinuch*."

"Shmuel Yaakov," he said, "just realize that *chinuch* is very different from any other endeavor. One must be absolutely certain that he wants to be a *mechanech* before he becomes one. If you have any doubts about whether or not you want to be a *mechanech*, well, you should probably look elsewhere," he told me with a wisdom I was hardly able to appreciate fully at the time.

I mulled over my *rosh yeshivah*'s words and mistakenly concluded that what they meant was that *chinuch*, in light of its innate holiness, required absolute devotion. A mind riddled with doubt cannot suit the loftiness of the pursuit of Jewish education. I figured that he was speaking in defense of the timeless task itself, warning that it was not proper to approach such a noble calling with even the slightest hesitation.

Years later I remembered the words of my rebbe, and it dawned on me that he was speaking in defense, not only of the tasks of *chinuch*, but also of his naive young *talmid*. It became suddenly plain that he meant something very different. The trials and tests of being a Jewish educator would be so intense, he was warning me, that unless I was absolutely certain that this was the field for me, I should not enter it. Only absolute certainty would see me through the difficult chapters of life as a *mechanech*. Otherwise I might be forever afflicted with misgivings and regrets.

I suppose the question that would logically find its way into this exact spot in my exposition is "Well, do you have regrets?" In all honesty I feel I may have had an easier go of things had I chosen something else, but that is not the same as saying I have regrets. Sure, occasionally I glance at friends, acquaintances, and former classmates, some of whom have gone on to be extremely successful (and I'm measuring success here in terms of dollars and cents) in assorted vocations and fields, and I wonder whether they haven't done better for themselves than I have. Sure, many are the days on which I come home after a long and taxing day in school and I say to my wife, quietly so that my children will not hear, *chas v'shalom*, "That's it. I've had it. There must be a better way of putting bread on the table." Many are the moments when I am so frustrated that I am ready to ignite, and I look in the mirror with very little love of self and think, *You must be some sort of lunatic. Couldn't you have picked something more simple to give your life to, something less risky — like being a kamikaze pilot or a mountain climber?*

Then, at more relaxed times, I become more contemplative, and I say that I am really very fortunate to be involved in a career that entails the utmost relevance and the highest spiritual gratification.

SO AT THE risk of being labeled schizophrenic, I would say that the issue of regret is determined largely by mood, by the time of day, by the last parental contact I had to initiate, or by a bunch of other incidentals.

And the issue is not whether I have regrets. The issue is what are the possible reasons that one might have regrets, if one were inclined to have regrets at all. I suppose, then, that what must follow is a description of some of the challenges involved in *chinuch*. Parents who will have occasion to speak to their son's rebbe or their daughter's *morah* will then have deeper insight into the teacher's mindset. How advantageous it could be for parents to have a more rounded glimpse into and appreciation for the factors with which *mechanchim* contend.

In addition, if any young hopeful has the opportunity to read this, he will automatically be in a more enlightened position to make the real choice, with, as my rebbe would have recommended, absolute certainty.

It might be thrown back at me that I should give the more positive side of the issue an equal chance, and that if I do not, this will be a one-sided and narrow view to the subject. Well, there will be plenty of the positive stuff later on in this work. The truth, is, however, that the merits of being a *mechanech* are well known and obvious. No writer is needed to come to the defense of the precious and innately rewarding work of the *Ribbono shel Olam* and the teachings of His Torah. So consider this one-sided approach as an initiation test, like the fabled fraternity initiation tests, which will separate between the informed parent and the parent who might not know how much effort a good teacher is investing in his or her child.

It will also perhaps weed out the limp and less than completely dedicated candidates from the field. In fact, *chinuch* itself will benefit from this inadvertent screening process. So read on, and make either an educated choice or a balanced self-evaluation when it's all over.

So What Are You in Now?

As a *mechanech*, I have often been asked a question that has never failed to send a chill down my spine. When meeting an acquaintance I have not seen for some time, somewhere after the preliminary *shalom aleichem*s, I might be asked, "So are you still in *chinuch*?" or "So what are you doing now?"

Now what exactly is that question supposed to mean? "Are you still in *chinuch*?" tends to conjure up in my mind other similar-sounding questions, like "So do you still have that ear infection?" or "Do you still live in that one-bedroom apartment with your fourteen children?"

Sure, it's more than likely that the questioner intends no malice. "Are you still in *chinuch*?" is a question that, in the minds of most, makes perfect sense, because *chinuch* is perceived as something temporary or transitional, not a serious, long-term "career" choice.

Alternatively, I do not believe that it would enter people's minds to ask, "So are you still practicing medicine?" or "Are you still in law?" Most of us would not even consider asking a businessman whether he is still in business (despite recessions and other financial worries) or whether he is still in that particular business. *Chinuch*, on the other hand, is something else entirely. It seems to breed such queries.

WHAT I HAVE noticed is that when it comes to the field of *chinuch* there appears to be an outrageous circularity. It is difficult, as with most circular tendencies, to pick a starting point, but let's try this.

A *mechanech* typically earns less than a desirable income. After a number of years he develops the sickly feeling, as his children increase in number, *baruch Hashem*, and as the available square footage of breathing space at home decreases at the same pace, that life tends to get more difficult with time. Thus, for financial reasons, many *melamdim* opt out of *chinuch* after some time, seeking their destinies and fortunes in other walks of life.

Chinuch is thus plagued with sizable yearly staff turnover in many institutions, and it thus holds forth little attraction for the young and hopeful, and perhaps most talented, prospective teachers. Often, then, the most ambitious and capable young *ben Torah* chooses a life somewhere beyond the cheder or yeshivah walls. He ends up with the perspective of an outsider, who, either because he never considered *chinuch* as a vocational option or because he consciously rejected it, views the entire field — and its practitioners — with some degree of disdain.

Thus much of the world "out there" approaches the realm of Jewish education with this predisposition of controlled condescension. So when it comes to determining the financing of schools, those lay people who must make the decisions do so with a slightly negative eye. The result is that Torah institutions must operate on very restricted and often less than adequate budgets. The end result of that, of course, is that a *mechanech* cannot be paid in accordance with either the importance of his task or his needs, earning a less than desirable income. This brings us right back to our assumed starting point.

Now, that may have been somewhat oversimplified, since there are several other factors that come into play. Still, the *melamed* is generally not the object of envy on the part of most observers. (Unless it is during vacation. One layman observed that there are two reasons he would love to be an educator: July and August.) So they innocently ask the question "Are you still in *chinuch*?" without realizing that their query can devastate the devoted *mechanech*, who is more than likely already laboring under the pressures in his life and his job. Hearing the question repeatedly is a sure-fire motive for him to leave the field "once and for all."

Financial Plight

The financial aspects of being in *chinuch* are without doubt the most disconcerting, for a variety of reasons.

I remember vividly a discussion I had a number of years ago with the head of a tuition committee serving a school that demanded tuition of its teachers, albeit with a hidden sense of mercy. (What was most curious, incidentally, was that the teachers were also forced to enroll their own children only in that school.) He said, "Listen, we all have to live up to our obligations. After all, Ploni is having a lousy year in his law practice. He must be earning under fifty thousand dollars this year, and he's still not coming to us asking for any subsidies. He's paying thousands in *sechar limud*."

That was quite a number of years ago, when a *melamed* was happy to be making under twenty thousand. I could not help thinking, *Good grief! What happens to be a lousy year for your lawyer friend is a year that surpasses the wildest fantasy of anyone in chinuch dreaming of having a good year.*

Several years after that, when spiraling inflation had increased incomes at nearly the same rate as the cost of living, an article in one of Canada's leading news magazines was brought to my attention. Statistics Canada (the arm of the Canadian government created with the aim of illustrating to Canadians just how abnormal they are) revealed the findings of a study of average family incomes in Canada. An average family of four was enjoying at that time an income of about fifty-two thousand dollars — even assuming that both spouses were working. Ostensibly a family of four enjoying (and that term is being used with reservation) less than that was therefore having to get by on less than the average.

Now consider the unique costs of living that the Torah-observant Jew must bear — kosher food, school tuition fees, making Pesach, twice a year having to purchase a moderate portion of the inventory of a children's shoe store — and the fact that most families among observant Jews have on the average eight members rather than four. One is easily led to the conclusion that a good deal more than the fifty-two thousand dollars that is the average in Canada is required. Moreover, considering that fifty-two thousand dollars substantially exceeded what most people in *chinuch* were earning when the study was published, one has little difficulty seeing that *mechanchim* were living near or below the poverty line. (I wonder if that's what people mean when they say things like "That poor guy is a *melamed*.")

Another disheartening aspect to a teacher's financial situation is that it is public domain. The *melamed*, among other public figures, walks around with a price tag affixed to his nose. Since a person's esteem is often directly proportional to the money owned and earned by the object of the esteem, a *mechanech*'s public esteem, and likely his self-esteem, too, will suffer.

MORE CRUCIAL IS the absence of that mystique most others enjoy, the mysterious question marks that surround one's whole being like an aura: "What do you think he makes a year?" "Say, I wonder how much that guy earns." A *melamed*'s proverbial laundry hangs out to dry in full view.

Somehow I have the feeling that if the Jewish educator were among those who earned a higher income, he could almost tolerate having his financial affairs be public knowledge. It certainly seems to be that unfortunate combination of low to middle income together with being financially sized up openly in the public sector that sends the hearts of so many of us crashing through the floor.

In turn, that issue is obviously tied to the depressing reality that so many people in society measure the worth of other individuals according to wealth or the lack of it. I have no desire to use these lines to pontificate about this. Nevertheless, this is a reality and psychologically a potentially difficult one for the educator to swallow. (Undoubtedly the same misgivings are felt by anyone who finds himself on the lower end of the financial spectrum.)

It must come as quite a shock, then, to the person who, steeped in idealism, feels that he will join the ranks of mankind's elite, the vanguard of the Jewish people, and then discovers that many others do not necessarily share the same opinion.

I suppose the other side of the issue should also be shared. The financial straits of the educator are not really all that different from those in many other fields. It is also argued that a *melamed* can do numerous things "on the side" — run a summer camp, teach private lessons, take on an additional position. Still, when all is said and done, the universal feeling among teachers is that life is a fiscal struggle.

The Problem of Being Exact

Let's take a look at a concern more intrinsically related to teaching that fills the heads and the lives of Jewish educators.

When I was a young boy of bar mitzvah age, I was privileged to have as a rebbe a Jew who was reputed as being one of the best teachers in town. In fact, he was a vibrant *chassidishe melamed* who brought every lesson to life with animation, humor, and unparalleled zest. Years later, after I had been away at yeshivah, I bumped into him at a wedding. I had not seen him in all those years, but I recognized him instantly, though he looked very different. Whereas his long and bushy beard had been jet black when he taught me in the eighth grade, it had turned white over the years.

Excitedly (for I, like all my classmates, had truly loved him) I approached him and said, *"Shalom aleichem."* On a whim I ventured, perhaps too boldly, "Rebbe, what happened to your beard?"

At once he sported his hallmark smile, all-knowing but mischievous, which had so endeared him to us. He pointed to his beard and said, "I'll tell you what happened. Every one of these white hairs is a *talmid*." Then, separating one lonely wisp of hair from the rest, he added, "Here, Klein, this one is you!"

The feeling I felt exuding from him at that moment was love, the type that is engendered by the unique bond between a rebbe and his *talmidim*. But the message in his words also made a dent in my mindset, and I stored it away for implementation with my own students.

DO NOT MISINTERPRET. I did not derive from his words that his life as a teacher had been stressful because of the challenges he faced in his work. Yes, *chinuch* is very demanding, but if one invests the effort necessary to be a good *mechanech*, it is also tremendously rewarding.

As I reflected on the demands, I felt that one of the greatest is that it entails painstaking exactness and commitment. That can be a real drain on one's energy and youthfulness. There are positive aspects to the stress, which stem from the wonders of the job, but they are stressful nonetheless.

I once attended a teacher's staff meeting during which the principal passed around a self-examination form for the teachers to evaluate themselves for excellence. It included a typical checklist of teaching proprieties, the dos and don'ts that make for a good teacher. But before we were instructed to complete the forms and test ourselves, the principal suggested that the objective was not just to get a good mark; rather, it was to get as close to perfect as possible. "We are like surgeons," he explained. "If a surgeon has an eighty-five percent success rate, he is not really doing very well. We, too, as educators, are dealing with the lives of children. An eighty-five percent may be a good test grade, but here it is not good enough."

At that dramatic point, one of the teachers interjected, "But the truth is we are in a far worse position than surgeons. A surgeon can bury his mistakes, while we have to speak to the parents about ours." When the laughter subsided, we were left with the understanding that a teacher must avoid errors just like the surgeon.

It is no wonder that my eighth-grade rebbe attributed his hairs to us, his students.

THE COUNTER-ARGUMENT to this is that every trade or profession requires exactness. Imagine a carpenter who constructs furniture without exactness or an architect who uses approximation in his blueprints or a surgeon, for that matter, who operates without being exact. Not very pleasing thoughts. Why, then, do I single out the teaching profession as the one that labors under the burden of this particular requisite of precision?

The reason is that precision and exactness alone are not enough for a person to be...precise and exact in this profession. Even if the teacher tries to be very exacting, he finds himself in compromising predicaments. And the reason for that is that the final evaluation is beyond his own control, lying rather within the jurisdiction of others. Allow me to explain. I can think of a couple of examples.

Once I was teaching the concept of *"Kadeish atzmecha b'muttar lach* — Sanctify yourself with that which is permitted to you" (*Yevamos* 20a). I chose the example of *chalav akum* to make the point that even if one may find dispensations or halachic opinions that hold that it is not absolutely necessary to be strict about *chalav Yisrael* in all circumstances, it may be considered proper to do so. I said to my students that although milk provided by a non-Jew is not nearly as much a problem today as *treif* meat, for many Jews the spirit of *"kadeish atzmecha"* will lead them to almost an identical sense of strictness.

A couple of days later my principal brought to my attention a complaint he had received from a parent, who took exception to the fact that "Rabbi Klein was equating the use of *chalav akum* with eating *chazir.*" I explained what I had really said, but that was anticlimactic for me. What was vital was the lesson I learned: a *melamed* cannot be too careful about what he says and the way in which he expresses himself.

On another occasion I was discussing with my class the idea of *galus*, Jewish exile. One point that was made was that the entire people are in *galus*, even those living in Israel, because there cannot be a real end to *galus* until the redemption.

A couple of weeks later, at a bar mitzvah, I got accosted — not even by a parent of one of my students, but by a friend of a parent — over the fact that I had the gall to tell my students that there was no difference between living in Israel and living in *chutz la'aretz*. I quickly proceeded to clarify that though I was not particularly Zionistic, even I could not possibly have expressed such a ludicrous thought. Suspiciously, and halfheartedly, the gentleman accepted my explanation. But there again I was reminded of the exactness we teachers cannot properly effect due to the misinterpretation that tags along with almost anything we say in a classroom.

IN TRUTH, OUR Sages alluded to the problem when they wrote, "*Chachamim hizharu b'divreichem...* — Wise ones, be careful with your words..." (*Avos* 1:11). They undoubtedly considered the possibility that students may miss the point or misinterpret or possibly even intentionally distort the real meaning or intention of what has been said. It is an occupational hazard of major proportions for teachers and needs to be borne in mind.

It also seems that the problem gets compounded with the age of the students. Teenage students tend to be opinionated about almost any topic a teacher might speak about. Therefore they tend to hear what they imagined you were going to say instead of what you did say.

Among the matters about which they are opinionated is the teacher's line of thinking. They believe they have the rebbe all figured out. So no matter what one actually says, one is at risk of being perceived as having said something else — something that conforms with what they imagined was said.

Another aspect that complicates the matter is the teacher's strength of character. If the teacher has presence, a strong personality, and as a result has a great influence over his students, he is in greater danger of being misinterpreted and judged unfairly.

Yes, the question of exactness surely is an issue with

many, if not all, professions, but it is not quite so removed from the personal control of the practitioner of the profession as it is with the educator. The carpenter, the architect, and the surgeon are really the masters of their own exactness. Not so the *melamed*.

Part Three

ORIENTATION

Introduction

Chances are that if you have reached this point in the book, you might actually be interested in the nature of the task of education. Well, as with many other endeavors, with *chinuch* there is an aspect of science and an aspect of art. *Science* denotes a systemized knowledge of a particular study, while *art* is its skilled application to a human purpose or goal.

One need not be even remotely considering a future in the field of *chinuch* to be curious about both its art and its science. There is an entire complex of thought and orientation one must consider in order to gain meaningful insight into Jewish education. There is little doubt that tomorrow's students will benefit from parents and teachers who are more astute and more aware of the rules of the game.

It's Not Just Curriculum!

When education becomes bogged down by unadulterated academics, it begins to lose its vitality and perhaps its self-justification. Education must be much more than simply imparting information to students; it must include an attempt to fashion character and to promote inherent change in students.

This might depend entirely on the type of learning that constitutes the vehicle of study. Studies that are undertaken for their extrinsic values — building functional or vocational skills, for example — may be carried on without the attempt to build character. However, learning undertaken for its inherent merit must be, by virtue of that very intrinsic good, directed at effecting mental and spiritual growth in students.

Limudei kodesh, for instance, must be taught with a partial orientation toward influencing students to change. If not, these studies become stripped of their *kedushah*. (Later on there will be a more detailed analysis of the distinctions between *limudei kodesh* and *limudei chol*.)

In one scenario I was teaching a full Torah curriculum as set out by the particular school. I detected instantly that there was no provision within the curricular guidelines for the teaching of *mussar, hashkafah*, or what is often referred to as *Yahadus*. Looking for some way of injecting these character-building studies into the program, I concluded that in *safah* (Hebrew language) and *dikduk* (Hebrew grammar), which were at the time part of the curriculum I had to teach and were also separate subjects in that particular system, I might choose a conducive text for our study.

I chose the introduction and the first two chapters of the classic *Mesilas Yesharim* as a vehicle for teaching sentence structure and vocabulary enrichment — but also for generating fundamental discussions about life's concerns and spiritual requirements. After doing this for a couple of years, I was summoned by my superiors and advised that "*safah* is *safah*" and it should not be used for "other things." *Mesilas Yesharim* was yanked from my program.

When I asked why there was no *Yahadus* program, I was informed that Torah learning is all the *Yahadus* that is required and that it needs no reinforcement from *mussar shmuessen*. The Torah speaks most eloquently for itself.

That argument sounded so impressive at first, until I paused to wonder what it might mean to the giants of *mussar* and Chassidus, who all felt that "straight" Torah study must be augmented by a more direct approach to building a Jewish heart.

I'LL NEVER FORGET a remark shared with me by a visitor to that same school. As the one in charge of inviting guest *rabbanim* to speak at various school functions, such as Rosh Chodesh assemblies, I invited a certain Rabbi T., relatively new in town, the head of one of the city's other Torah schools since six months previously. He came, he spoke, and when he finished he came up to me to introduce himself. "So you're Rabbi Klein."

"Yes" was all I could muster at the moment, trying to swallow the strange lump that had formed in a flash inside my throat. I could not help but wonder, *Uh-oh, what has he heard about me?*

"I must share an interesting episode with you, because it pertains to you," he continued.

"Really," I replied, bracing myself.

"We have this girl, Leah, in our eleventh-grade class," began Rabbi T.

"Yes, I remember her. She used to be a student of ours," I answered.

"Right. Well, a couple of months ago I noticed that she seemed to be slacking off — in her learning, in her attendance at davening, in her *menschlichkeit*." I wondered why he was telling me this. I found out soon enough. "One day I got so fed up with her that I went up to her and asked her what was going on with her, why the slouching. So she told me that when she started to weaken a bit in school and in *Yiddishkeit* she noticed that no one — not the principal, not her teachers — approached her to find out what was happening. 'I figured nobody really cares, so I just let myself go more and more,' she said. At that point I challenged her reasoning.

I told her, 'Leah, you're an eleventh-grade student. You need to be reminded of your obligations? You need to be constantly prodded and pushed?' You know what she answered me? She said, 'You should know that when I was in ninth grade I had a teacher named Rabbi Klein. If it hadn't been for his constant *mussar* shmoozes and prodding and pushing, then I probably would not have even ended up at this school. I probably would have gone to public high school.' I was floored by her answer, and I was waiting for the opportunity to meet you so I could tell you about it."

After the assembly, I considered going into the office of the principal to share the episode with him in the hope of convincing him that there is a need and a purpose in making *Yahadus* more of an active undertaking instead of merely a process akin to osmosis. But I decided against it.

I ended up restoring *safah* to what had been intended by the one who devised the curriculum, but I turned to our Friday study of *parashas hashavua* as the opportunity to include the "frontal *Yiddishkeit*" approach. After briefly reviewing the highlights of the parashah, I would seize on one particular aspect and use it as a springboard for discussions of crucial Torah themes, all with the aim of providing *chizuk* and *hisorerus*.

One day I happened to mention this shift in approach to my principal. I was curious to see how he would react. He was silent, and to this day I'm not certain what he was thinking. Was he just so exasperated with me that he felt it was useless to take issue with me again? Or was he acquiescing because he secretly agreed with me? I'm not sure, but I hope it was the latter.

I SHOULD QUALIFY a point I made earlier. I suggested that the need to infuse learning with character building largely depends on the nature of the study. In other words, *middos* training will be an integral part of *limudei kodesh*, whereas it may not be as crucial in general studies. When I reflect on the matter again, however, I am not entirely certain that this is so.

I recall one day urging a certain general studies teacher on my staff to use the classic approach known as roleplaying to show a young bully in his class the folly of his ways. Apparently the teacher went a bit too far and made a dent (a richly deserved one, mind you) in the boy's self-concept. His mother, to whom the young charge promptly complained, paid me a visit together with her husband, a noted rabbinical figure in our community.

The dialogue that transpired at that meeting was itself the stuff of which tragicomedy is made, but that is not important here. What is crucial is that at some point the husband declared that the role of the English teacher really does not include building *middos*. That area belongs exclusively to the rebbe.

Well, in the course of time, that opinion has come to receive mixed reviews in my mind. In one sense *middos* as a course of study belongs — and, yes, exclusively — to the religious studies portion of the day. On the other hand, the general studies portion must include the facility to promote, albeit using different venues, some measure of character training, too. The old adage says that nature abhors a vacuum. If there is a vacuum, or even a potential vacuum, of personality building during the several hours of the day that general studies might be taught, it may result in negative character development or the deterioration of proper *middos*.

Practically this means a couple of things. First and foremost, an English teacher cannot be employed if he might instill bad traits in his students. Second, he must himself be a model of positive character traits, since he will be serving as a role model, even inadvertently, and since he will have to deal with situations — in the classroom, in the schoolyard, in the lunch area — where he will have to arbitrate and guide in the areas of *middos*. It can thus be said that teaching *middos* is part of the general studies teacher's role, too.

The only problem is that I would like to know where to find the reservoir of human resources that houses all those people who are capable, willing, and available to teach general studies and who are also suitable as potential role models for children to emulate in their character-building process.

That addresses an entirely separate issue, one we will deal with later on.

Equitability and Nepotism

There should be a clear dichotomy between the educational function of a school and its financial arm. In other words, an educator — and this includes the principal — should not be involved in all aspects of a school's fiscal affairs. There are some financial aspects the educator might have access to, for example, fund-raising. However, when it comes to tuition and specific amounts being paid by specific parents, *mechanchim* should not be privy to this information (though sometimes it may be obvious).

Several years ago a senior student became involved in a dispute (I grace the silliness that it was by referring to it as such) with another boy from his class. As is usually the case, the solution to the dispute lay somewhere between the two stated positions. As the principal, I was called on to summon the same wisdom as Shlomo HaMelech that every principal is presumed to possess and to arbitrate the difference of opinion. Acting according to the grandest rabbinical traditions of compromise, I worked out a settlement between the two young litigants, which approximated my view of *emes* in the case.

No sooner had I patted myself on the back for a job well done when I received an urgent buzz from the school secretary in the main office (yes, sometimes the buzz itself sounds urgent!). It was the mother of one of the two boys.

"Rabbi Klein," she began.

"Good afternoon, Mrs. A. How are you?" I started in cleverly.

"I wanted to tell you that we did not approve of the way you handled that fight our son had with...that other boy," she challenged.

My first thought was that I must remind our secretary once again that she should not allow the students to use the school phone as often as she obviously was permitting.

"To tell you the truth, Mrs. A., it's often impossible to decipher the truth in some cases. Often we are left with no choice but to exercise a compromise between two students," I explained, rather thoughtfully I thought.

"Rabbi Klein, you should know that my husband and I pay *full* tuition, whereas that other boy's parents couldn't possibly — his father is in *kollel* or something. I really think that we are entitled to a little bit of consideration," she insisted.

"Mrs. A., I do not know who pays what. Nor do I want to know, nor do I care. Every boy is a student of equal standing, and frankly I think you are abusing the *Ribbono shel Olam*'s blessings by throwing it around in this way. Just because you are fortunate enough to have the ability to do what you are obligated to do by paying full tuition does not mean..." And I escalated to a sermon that would surely have been the envy of any of the great *mashgichim*.

"Well, I'm going to speak to my husband about this," said Mrs. A., clearly unconvinced by my tirade. "He'll give you a call."

The fact that the husband did not give me a call illustrated to me that he probably did not share his good wife's unique sense of ethics and justice.

But then this important idea occurred to me: with human beings being as they are, it is feasible that educators may fall under the influence of the almighty tuition dollar if they know too much. It is really best, then, that educators are not made privy to that type of information.

There is another sort of nepotism in the world of *chinuch*, and that is the tendency for positions to be offered to people with special pull. But that is a fact in every walk of life, not only in *chinuch*, so I will omit a commentary.

I feel it is vital, however, to conclude that for the most part the parents with whom I have dealt over the years have exercised wisdom and understanding and have portrayed nothing like what has been described here.

Middos and Derech Eretz

A very problematic feature of Torah education is a gaping hole in *middos* and *derech eretz* (MDE), refinements of character and interpersonal skills, on the part of the children of the very *frum* families — not as individuals, and not in isolation, but rather when they are together in groups. This has been observed by a wide array of people — from *mechanchim* to parents, from the most observant Jews to the occasional non-Jew employed in a Torah school, from key players in *chinuch* to the most impartial observers. In fact, it has even been suggested that the more *frum*, the greater the weakness in MDE.

It is not without a tremendous heaviness of heart that I allow myself to even make this suggestion. It is a scathing indictment of fellow Jews who are *yere'im* and *sheleimim*. At the same time, however, it might be so. And if it is so, we are certainly compelled to discover why.

Before continuing, I want to acknowledge that this topic is intensely inflammatory, but I grapple with the topic not as an outside observer looking askance at others, but rather as an insider, burdened by the truth of these observations. I do not approach the topic as a casual and callous analyst, but as one eager to explain and fathom what is apparently a most distasteful feature of the Torah *chinuch* scene. So, that having been said, the question in a nutshell is, why is it that the children of the very *frum* families are lacking in MDE?

ONE EDUCATOR OFFERED a feeble attempt at humor to explain. When the Creator called the Jews to receive the Torah at Sinai, all the very observant ones began running wildly, pushing, shoving, and shouting to secure a piece of the holy Torah. By the time the more coolly disposed and relaxed, less observant Jews arrived on the scene, there was only one small piece left — the tractate of *Derech Eretz*. Thus they were left with MDE alone.

Beyond the arrogance and chauvinism that underlies this joke, there is a serious rational flaw. If MDE is an integral part of Torah, as it most surely is, why didn't highly enthused observant Jews grab at it as much as they did the other parts of Torah? *Menschlichkeit* is also part of the Torah (this is why *Pirkei Avos* commences with "Moshe received the Torah from Sinai," according to the Maharal et al.) and should have been embraced at least as much as the laws of kashrus and Shabbos. In fact, since "*derech eretz kadmah laTorah — derech eretz* comes before Torah," it should have been embraced even more.

What are some other, real explanations for this phenomenon?

Mr. Avi Shulman, a noted *mechanech*, once pointed

out that while the school may be responsible for imparting academic learning to its students with the parents reinforcing it, it is the role of parents to impart and develop MDE skills in children with the school reinforcing those. Few would question this fundamental premise. When it comes to *menschlichkeit*, those who must take responsibility, and therefore accountability, are none other than the parents. So if there is a breakdown in the MDE development of children today, we must look to the parents.

If only all teachers were proper examples of MDE. Alas, many are not. Yet a lack of MDE on the part of a teacher, albeit as reprehensible a phenomenon as a similar shortcoming in a parent, is less a cause for devastation. The reason is that even in the best of circumstances *mechanchim* make less of an impact in the development of children's personalities than parents do.

Some would argue that this position is a cop-out and that the school should also take charge of imparting MDE skills to children. Personally I would go along with that sentiment — to an extent. A school can teach *middos* just as it can teach the thirty-nine *melachos*. A school can launch a *derech eretz* campaign just as it can a *berachos* bee. Still, those kinds of endeavors fall into the realm of reinforcement of the *menschlichkeit* hopefully being developed at home. It is extremely rare for a school to have the capacity to effect character building from scratch (unless, of course it is a boarding school, or, *Rachmana litzlan*, an orphanage).

Most people have some awareness of this. Almost every time I have spoken to a parent concerning his or her child's misbehavior or MDE weakness, the parent feels somehow — probably subconsciously — compelled to apologize to me that the child behaved in that way. Now why would parents apologize if not for the subconscious realization that they, through their parenting, have effected their children's MDE strengths and weaknesses?

The sound assumption, then, is that parents are the ones who teach *menschlichkeit* skills. Without any further ado, then, let us consider a number of the problems that can be engendered, wittingly or otherwise, by today's parents.

ONE CASE COMES immediately to mind. Years ago I had to call a mother because her son — let's call him Meir — was terrorizing another boy in his class. Apparently the second child — let us call him Chaim — was the brunt of an endless chain of snide comments and taunts. The reason was that Chaim had transferred to our yeshivah from another one. As a newcomer, Chaim was put through a relentless initiation at Meir's hands. Chaim came home each evening after school and, more often than not, broke down crying over the emotional ordeal he had been forced to withstand that day. When Chaim's mother could bear no more, and all her advice to her son to ignore it and rise above it failed, she called me and asked if I could intervene.

There are a number of things that can be done in such a scenario. Personally I felt that since this was an MDE problem, the first thing I should do was contact Meir's parents. My assumption was that they would be only too eager to rectify the matter and see to it that their offspring learned to be more considerate of others' feelings.

I was wrong. When I presented the situation to the mother, I was thunderstruck by her response. "Well, you know, Rabbi Klein, we have always taught Meir to be selective about the friends he keeps and the relationships he has. I'm not sure that this Chaim boy, being that he transferred from *that* school, is the kind of boy I would want Meir to hang around with."

I tried to collect a modest bit of composure and said to her, "It may be a good thing to encourage a bit of discrimination in the tastes of your child, but certainly you would not approve of your child hurting another boy simply because he came from a different school. And just because a child is not exactly one's friend is no excuse to victimize him."

"They're only children," she retorted, "and it's very difficult to teach them limits. For me the important thing is that he be selective of his friends."

Yes, this conversation (like all the conversations recorded here) really did take place. I am inventing nothing.

Back to the point. How much MDE can Meir be expected to have if his mother, and probably his father as well, openly encourage an unbridled selectivity even if it incurs the expense of another person's feelings?

(By the way, I never did succeed in convincing the mother about the need to curtail her son's demolition exercises, but I did manage to get through to Meir himself.)

Then there was another rather nasty situation I had to deal with. There was a boy — let me call him Velvel — who had a particularly malodorous personal hygiene problem. It seems he was not very fond of showering, nor was he convinced of the importance of changing clothing from time to time. As a result, some of the boys in his class took a distinct dislike to him, making unkind remarks about him behind his back and even to his face. They also approached one of the teachers of the class with a complaint that it was impossible to sit near him, for the obvious reason.

Now, the fact that the boys in Velvel's class were making fun of him was definitely a manifestation of a collective weakness in MDE, but my judgment in the matter was that the root of the difficulty was in Velvel's personal deficiency. This is what had to be tended to, at least for expedience's sake.

I called Velvel's mother to discuss the very sensitive matter, knowing how painful it might be for her to hear her son's principal saying what I had to say. But I reasoned that if I were the parent involved, what I would want most would be to be made aware of the situation.

Velvel's mother was not at all upset or insulted at my report — at least, that was my perception at my end of the line. She explained that Velvel was now old enough — ten(!) — to look after his personal hygiene and the clothing he chose to wear. (I forgot to add earlier that the trousers he wore were pathetically short and soiled.) I was right, she said, in trying to deal with the problem, and she wished, she said, that Velvel would develop the necessary life skills to be "on top of it all."

I suggested politely that Velvel might be a bit too young to have to deal with these responsibilities and that it might be more appropriate for her to help him along in the morning. But Velvel's mother was a mother of more than ten children, and, she said, she knew exactly how to raise children so that they would develop properly.

Poor Velvel. He had to go it alone. I took Velvel under my wing — not a simple thing to do — and with limited success achieved a change in his personal bearing, and a slight change was evident in the way the other boys felt about him.

His problem was an MDE issue, and I felt that his well-intentioned mother was largely to blame for it.

AS I APPROACH the next point, I want to once again pause to interject a word of apology to the reader. What I am about to write could appear to be very controversial, and quite possibly heretical. It is not — as I will explain during the course of the polemic.

One of the factors in the MDE equation is that the more *frum* tend to have large families, and this can have an adverse effect on the children's *middos* development. It is wonderful thing, a blessing of unparalleled dimension. But the blessing, as marvelous as it is, presents a challenge of its own, one that bears a price tag for parents as well as for the children themselves, that we should be aware of.

The first problem is simply a quantity-related problem. Parents have a certain amount of hours (or minutes!) per day to devote to their children. Simple rules of division mean that the more children there are, the less time each child will be allotted by the parents. It is a safe premise that a parent needs to devote time to his children's academic and psychological growth. The obvious conclusion is that the more children there are in a family, the more difficult it might be for them to become models of MDE.

Here, too, there are counter-arguments of which I am perfectly aware. Too much parental involvement in a child's development can dwarf or stifle the child's growth. Therefore, it would be argued, if there are many children in a family, it is actually more likely that the children will develop in a wholesome manner due to the fact that their parents are less disposed to muddle up their lives. Also, when there are numerous children in the family, the older ones are encouraged to assist the younger ones with work, responsibilities, and personal growth. This alleviates some of the pressure from the parents, and it provides the older children in the family with the opportunity for their own special development that other young people their age might not have.

Alternatively, in this area of life, as in so many others, the question of balance and moderation comes into play. We are not talking about parents who drive their kids crazy by being overbearing, overinvolved, and overprotective. We are referring to parents who have a balanced approach to parenting. When the Creator grants them the wonderful fortune of having many children, I urge them to keep their aim trained on the target constantly — ensuring that each child be made to feel that he is unique and special in some way.

This brings me to the second potential pitfall. A child who contends with a house full of siblings develops certain social skills that help him survive in the family environment. Since there is probably — in addition to a limit on the time parents have to devote to the child — a limitation of various other things, such as space, attention, material resources (and corner pieces of chocolate cake with flowers on it), the atmosphere might be tainted with jealousy and competitiveness. It is all a child can do to meet the many challenges to his emotional survival at home, apart from the academic and social pressures at school. So the way he survives is by developing certain social skills and senses.

Some of these may be good, like the ability to communicate and to compromise and share. Some, on the other hand, may be undesirable in a social setting, like the ability to deceive, to win, to control, to vanquish. A child who picks up such negative behavior at home might come to school and manifest it in his interaction with his peers and classmates. Hence MDE weakness can emanate from having many siblings at home — unless parents are attuned to the challenges and exercise wisdom in dealing with them.

Yes, certainly in many large families each child is a gem and a model of the best behavior. And, yes, it is well known that there are numerous social advantages to there being many children in a family. The older children develop parenting skills long before they are called on to be parents, for instance. Still, in my experiences, I have noted a greater tendency of MDE weakness in large families than in smaller families.

I certainly do not wish to create any false impressions. My singling out larger families as a potential cause for *middos* weakness is in no way implying that one should avoid having a large family. *Chalilah v'chas*! (In fact, I am the proud father of a rather large one myself.) I declare vehemently that this is in no way my intention. We Jews have always had large families. I'm just giving a word of caution to parents of large families. To such parents I would say, "Remember the extra responsibility that goes with it. Apportion your time and your concern equitably and thoughtfully, and remember that each of your children may be contending with psychological and emotional forces that will likely be more than he is able to handle with aplomb."

ANOTHER FACTOR MAY be the length of the school day. Most cheder children, for example, are in school for davening early in the morning and remain until five or six in the evening. The length of the day, combined with the rigorous demands made of them — social, academic, and physical — are often more than they can tolerate without incurring some side effects, such as tension and irritability.

By contrast, the child from a more modern framework may begin his day later and end it earlier. For him, school does not hold out the prospect of an overly demanding structure.

Again, does this mean that school ought to end earlier or that it is wrong to keep a child in front of his Gemara longer? It means nothing of the sort. However, it is a factor we should keep in mind when we struggle with the question of why the children seem to exhibit more negative behavior. It is possibly the result of the positive aspects of our lifestyle. We should be doing all we can to stem the imperfections in MDE, but we must understand the causes first. To be sure, fatigue and poor nutrition during the course of a school day can also contribute to behavioral difficulties. Parents and educators can work together in regulating the latter, and this type of cooperative effort should be promoted.

But let's return to parenting for a while; I haven't finished with that just yet. In fact, let us devote a whole chapter to the relationship between parents and teachers, since this seems to be an increasingly topical issue in our lives.

Cross-fire 1

In addition to being a "Jewish education professional," I have had for a number of years the pleasure of being the editor of Perspectives, a journal of Torah viewpoints published by the Agudath Israel of Canada. Every so often my two usually distinct callings overlap, and there appears an article relating to chinuch in the folios of Perspectives.

In the summer issue of 5754, I printed a piece entitled, somewhat innocently, "Dear Teacher: An Open Letter." It illustrates what may very well be a common attitude among parents.

Dear Teacher: An Open Letter

You may no longer remember me. After all, it is almost a decade since you last saw me, and the multitudes of students that you have taught could certainly eclipse one single individual from your memory. I, however, remember you very clearly. I remember many things you said to me and the feelings you expressed by word and gesture. Unfortunately these things are much more prominent in my mind than the subjects you actually taught me.

I wish I could say that your influence left me with many positive, uplifting feelings, that your love of learning and teaching motivated me to strive to my utmost to excel, that your feelings for your fellow man taught me to care and share, that your expressions of appreciation taught me the meaning of *hakaras hatov*, that your compassion taught me kindness, that your forbearance taught me patience and tolerance, and that your esteem for every human being taught me respect. For are these not the ideals of every genuine teacher?

Perhaps you were too young or inexperienced to realize that your kindness or lack of it would be remembered by your students long after graduation — into adulthood. Perhaps you didn't realize that some of the negative things you said would cause painful memories for always. You probably didn't realize how your bad moods affected me as a child — not just as a student — or how I felt when I lost marks unjustly because you were having a hard day.

You surely don't remember how I couldn't finish a test in time and how you wouldn't show any leniency by giving that extra time I needed, although I had studied for days. You certainly have forgotten about the marks you deducted because I forgot to underline the title or omitted the date, yet it never occurred to you to give me a bonus for answering that difficult question especially well. You most certainly could not have realized that your understanding of my grades because of your fear of overstating them put a blight on my enthusiasm to study. Someone once told me that *E* is for effort, but she must have gone to a different school.

You may not have appreciated that at that tender age my love of learning could so easily be extinguished because I felt your dislike or displeasure. You could not have imagined that my eagerness to go to school could be so totally dampened by one negative report card that I knew I did not deserve. Oh, how I longed for a good word, a show of approval for that project I worked so hard on. It hurt to be told, "You may take your seat," without hearing any word of commendation. I really couldn't understand why you so seldom gave us a smile. Of course, I was not mature enough to see that you had other things on your mind. All I knew was that you were our teacher, our role model, and I attempted to study and to gesture to seek your approval.

Of course, we weren't angels, and we did *shtick*, which deserved repercussions, but we were children and we expected you to understand and guide us with a firm and loving hand. I often felt the firmness — but where was the love?

I am writing to you because you are a teacher still, and one good word or otherwise can make it or break it for that student you may not have any special warm feeling for. But because you are a teacher, you have made an unspoken commitment to care for the spiritual and mental well-being of each of your students. This is a monumental task that no teacher can take lightly. It is truly difficult to teach with discipline and yet to show warmth and kindness with the rambunctious, often impudent, youth of today.

A large family or other responsibilities often lay heavy upon your shoulders. Yet, by being a teacher, these are things you must put aside. You must consider each of your sixty-seven students as a person and individual, even if you teach her only forty minutes a day. Whether it's *Chumash* or French, you are her role model. You are the person she looks up to and seeks to respect and emulate. The highest form of flattery is her wish to be like you. You must create the caring atmosphere that will induce her to follow your example.

Anger and punishment are not the only — or even necessarily the proper — modes of *chinuch*. Positive reinforcement, a bonus rather than a minus, a smile rather than a frown — can often accomplish tenfold. The former, however, may cause irreparable lifelong damage. The world says, "You can catch more flies with honey than with vinegar." You can undoubtedly nurture the love and devotion of your students with a good word rather than with criticism.

You surely forgot how you once embarrassed me in front of the whole class. I, however, can never forget. The old pain still jiggles the shadows of my memory.

You meant well, I'm sure. And yet I wish my memories were different. It's up to you to make them different for your pupils of '94.

                Yours faithfully,
                Your student of 19__

WELL, AS IS often the case with many of the articles that appear in my journal, the response to this particular piece was vehement and emotional. On the one hand, a number of parents heaped untold praises upon me for having the good sense to print such a piece. "I only hope that all the teachers in our schools read it," said one father with heartfelt concern. Another reported to me that when his wife read the letter she immediately thought of a particular teacher who had taught her daughter, and she was certain that that teacher must have been the one referred to in the article. I told the fellow to assure her that it could not possibly have been the case. I was not very convincing.

Then, one afternoon, a day or two after the issue of *Perspectives* reached the *frum* homes of Toronto, I was verbally accosted by a small but vocal delegation of *melamdim* as I entered my office in school. They charged that I was contributing to the deterioration of the view parents had of teachers by publishing the "garbage" contained in the letter. "You've set back the cause of educators twenty years," one suggested. I responded by saying that in all honesty there were — and are — educators in our system who can accurately be described by many of the phrases written in the letter and that there is no harm in being open and honest about it.

Actually, I had thought that the fact that I myself am an educator would shine a realistic light on the entire controversy. I shared this rationale that afternoon with my colleagues, but once again I was not very convincing.

And so it was day after day. It became a primary topic of discussion. Many were supportive of the letter, and many were not. As the editor I was treated to endless praises and almost endless grumbles. (As the editor, I suppose I must live with it. I have often been told that if one cannot tolerate the smell of gunpowder, he ought to stay away from the battle.)

Secretly I felt that it was a pity no educator was submitting a parallel letter portraying the other side of the issue. And as I bemoaned the absence of such a literary submission, I received a piece written by a Toronto educator, hand-delivered to my house. I read it, felt that it understated several points, overstated others, and entirely missed the mark on a few, but I decided that overall it hit the spot. So I printed it in the very next issue, while the controversy was still fairly fresh in the minds of my readers.

Dear Student: An Open Letter

I read with interest your letter in *Perspectives*. I can't be sure that your letter was directed at me, but it could have been, so I've decided to answer you, whoever you may be.

Of course teachers should be role models. Of course they should instill a love of learning. Of course they should never, ever be in a bad mood, regardless of their personal circumstances. Of course they should absolutely always be positive. Of course, of course...the list just goes on and on.

I once had a student meet me shopping in a supermarket. Her mouth dropped and she gasped, "*Morah!* You shop here, too?" Incredible! Teachers are actually flesh and blood. I suppose you could never have imagined the effect it had when your mother or father called me at home in the evening (without my consent) to complain and/or ask for an extension on that project and/or more time for you to study for the test that had been assigned a month before. Your mother began the conversation with "I figured you wouldn't mind that I called you at home." Well, with eight children of my own and a house to care for, I'm a bit exhausted by ten-thirty in the evening, when your mother called. Why on earth did she "figure" I wouldn't mind?

Did I ever once get a note of thanks or that proverbial pat on the back from either you or your parents? You probably never realized the sinking feeling I got day in and day out walking into your class, where the hostility was sometimes palpable. Oh, sure, there was the odd time that I got some positive feedback, but that was the exception rather than the rule.

Still, I suppose that, as a *mechaneches*, I'm supposed to be dedicated. Well, you know something? I am. But when I had to contend with your nervousness when your "dedicated" parents went to Florida during the winter, leaving you in Maria's loving care, I could not help wondering how dedicated they were.

Perhaps you don't realize that negativity breeds negativity. Certainly you could not have realized at your age how your attitude toward your schoolwork and thus toward me hampered my ability to see you in any other light. Each time you didn't take a test on time or hand in homework, although with another "legitimate" excuse, I guess you didn't realize how it wears a person (read: teacher) down.

You say in your letter that I once embarrassed you. In truth, you did not share with the readers how you actually embarrassed yourself with your inappropriate and disruptive behavior.

And who says that you "lost marks unjustly because I was having a bad day"? I don't remember you coming to ask me to explain. I only remember some mumbling under your breath. As for a report card that you did not deserve, who decides that? The student or the teacher?

But that is really another issue. It is not your fault that your parents let you know clearly that "the teacher is wrong." You are not to blame that your father told you, "I'll speak to a member of the board and fix that teacher," simply because he disagreed with something. It is not your fault that you had a hard time recognizing my authority when your parents did such a wonderful job undermining it.

Just like ordinary people, teachers have their ups and downs. Sometimes the chemistry with a student is wrong; personalities just don't click. Is it reasonable to assume that one negative school experience could really leave such deep emotional wounds that you express in your letter? It seems to me that these bitter feelings might have stemmed from ongoing clashes between you and your teachers throughout your school years.

You sign your name "Mrs." That means that you are old enough now to deal with life's adversities (I suppose). If you feel that I (or whoever) left you with "lifelong damage," I would suggest that you talk it out, if not with me, then with someone you trust. Honestly, it's not healthy to carry around all that baggage. Life is not always to our liking.

Remember, too, that if you have your own school-age children, these negative feelings can carry over to them and affect their own school experiences.

Yes, I did mean well, and, yes, I too wish my memories of your class were more pleasant.

I hope they will be with my class of '94.

Signed, Mrs. "U. Know-who"

If ever there were a clear illustration of the disparity between a teacher's point of view and that of a parent, I believe we have just seen it. In truth, I experience it on an almost daily basis, and I know that the issue is so central that it deserved a chapter unto itself.

Ethics for the Teacher

Beyond the technical aspects of education, teachers need to be concerned with the underlying spirit of education. Education is distinguishable from other occupations in that a positive spirit is fundamental to the whole operation. The teacher deals with children; he strives to shape them in both knowledge and attitude. He is not handling passive material, which is forever receptive to the whim and fancy of the arbiter. To an extent, there is an element of that, too, as Elisha ben Avuyah declared in the Mishnah: "He who learns as a child may be compared to ink written on new paper" (*Avos* 4:25). But there is more.

Each child is a unique and wonderful world of dreams and emotions, a complex amalgam of fears and infirmities, and he must be handled accordingly. This is every bit as integral to the teacher's suitability as the doctor's ability to diagnose a patient's symptoms. The teacher must desire to treat his students as human beings with all that this entails; he must, therefore, create a teaching spirit.

There has been for hundreds of years a serious problem the *melamed* has faced — one of image. The very term *melamed* was laced with a strongly stigmatic flavor. A *proste melamed*, a simple teacher, was the Yiddish accolade bestowed upon those whose fate had them teaching cheder. The negative feeling created by the stigma caused the teacher himself to wonder about his worth among men.

Fortunately for many, a large number of *melamdim* were able to triumph over this due to sheer commitment and dedication. Others, however, were unable to. As a result, their lack of inner peace was, and is, relayed to their students in a covert but very potent way. To a degree, the reason for the attitude toward teachers was related to the caliber of the teachers themselves.

It was quite common for a person who was incapable or unwilling to take up some other livelihood to become a *melamed*. There was a lack of a sense of mission that is so important in *chinuch*. Just as common was the sort of teacher whose only qualification was the fact that he knew the most elementary material and was deemed fit for the job. To a large measure, the aura surrounding *chinuch* was devoid of professionalism and purpose. It is thus easy to see why the *melamed* was deprived of social status and why, as a result, a certain loss of self-respect was incurred. The *melamed*'s acceptance into society *and* his suitability for the tasks were both lowered. What came first may be interesting but insignificant.

In recent years some of the status teachers ought to possess has been restored; *chinuch* has become professionalized. Terms like *moreh* and *morah* and *mechanech* have been substituted for *melamed* in an effort to revitalize the image. (Curiously, though, the Almighty Himself is called a *Melamed* [*Tehillim* 94:10], as was Moshe Rabbeinu [*Devarim* 4:1].) Today *chinuch* is considered a science in addition to an art; theories and policies abound.

The process, though, has ushered the Jewish teacher into another perspective altogether. In the course of modernizing Jewish education and society's view of it, many have lost the sense of spirit that is the very lifeblood of *chinuch*. They have perhaps achieved a partial goal, rendering *chinuch* as vital as any other occupation. But the means to this goal are not completely justifiable. They have stripped *chinuch* of many of the characteristics that make it distinct from all other occupations. It goes without saying that the teacher — be he a *mechanech* or a *melamed* — must be conscious of this distinctiveness constantly.

The Sages of the Gemara spoke most emphatically about teaching the *tinokos shel beis rabban*, the Jewish schoolchildren.

One passage alone contains three statements about it:

> Rabbi Yehudah said in the name of Rav: "What is meant by the verse 'Do not touch My anointed ones' (*Divrei HaYamim* I 16:22)? It refers to *tinokos shel beis rabban* [*tashbar*]." Rabbi Hamnuna said: "Yerushalayim was destroyed only because they suspended the schoolchildren." [This does not mean that children were expelled from school for bad behavior; it means they stopped teaching them.] And even such pronouncements are not to be compared to that of

Reish Lakish in the name of Rabbi Yehudah HaNassi: "The world is sustained only because of the breath of the schoolchildren [expelled when they learn Torah]."

(Shabbos 119b)

The Maharal explains (*Nesivos Olam, Nesiv HaTorah*, ch. 10) that Torah sustains the world, but the Torah of young children particularly sustains it even more, since it is the Torah of innocence. This is what Abayei meant when he explained to Rav Papa that the breath of the schoolchildren is "breath without sin." The teacher, writes the Maharal, brings unadulterated holiness into the world, a sanctity that is of the highest sort; it is beyond the physical incarnation, for it is of the intellect.

For this reason Reish Lakish proclaimed that we may not suspend Jewish education even for the reconstruction of the Beis HaMikdash. The sanctity of the Beis HaMikdash is lodged, as it were, in wood and stone, while the sanctity of *tashbar* is entirely incorporeal. Thus, besides the many social, nationalistic, historical, and cultural benefits wrought by Jewish education for the people of Israel, *chinuch* is the single most important activity in which one can be involved in a purely mystical sense. A person's self-image as a teacher needs no bolstering, his social status needs no revitalization, when viewed through the words of the Sages. The teacher can be involved in no nobler task because he helps to sustain the world itself. So while a teacher must regard himself as a practitioner of a specific set of technical acts, he must never lose sight of the sanctity of what he does.

Ethics for the Teacher

SO DISTINCT IS Jewish education from other sorts of livelihood that, according to the halachah, teachers must be viewed differently even with respect to salary. The original Talmudic ordinance (*Nedarim* 37a) was that the *melamed* may receive no remuneration whatsoever for his efforts. This does not imply that a teacher's work is a valueless commodity. On the contrary, it means that the work is priceless, not marketable. No price or wage can be ascribed to work that is priceless. Fixing a value to it would be a denigration of such work.

Later on, Rambam cites the revised Talmudic prescriptive:

> The teacher may receive payment for teaching Tanach in a place where this is the custom. This is prohibited for teaching the oral tradition, regardless of custom.
>
> *(Hilchos Talmud Torah 1:7)*

The basis for this is the verse, spoken by Moshe, "See I have taught you statutes and laws as God commanded me" (*Devarim* 4:5). The Sages interpret Moshe's words: "Just as I have taught with no financial reward, so shall you teach with no financial reward throughout the generations."

To be sure, fixing a monetary value to something limits its significance. The shoemaker earns less than the physician because they are both subject to the conceptions of the society in which they live. And the labors of both are restricted in social importance to the amounts of money they receive for their services. Salary is a measure of social acceptance. To box a teacher into a particular financial bracket is to put a specific value on the service he provides. This is offensive to the spirit of *chinuch*. Just as it would have appeared ridiculous for Moshe Rabbeinu to demand a salary for his teaching of Torah to Israel, so is it offensive today for teachers to receive a salary for teaching Torah to Israel, since today's *melamed* is a partial heir to the vocational heritage of Moshe.

Of course, such a spiritual formulation is very idealistic in the way it portrays the worth of a teacher, but it is not very practical. Sanctity alone will not feed and clothe the teacher's family; his creditors might prefer something a bit more substantial.

The *Shulchan Aruch* does make mention of a practice of paying teachers:

> The recent custom of paying teachers is permitted, since it is evident that [since he spends his time teaching] he puts aside other employment and business.
>
> *(Yoreh Deah 246:5)*

Thus salary for teachers has entered the framework of halachah, although it is not referred to as *sechar*, remuneration, but rather as *sechar batalah*, remuneration due to suspension from other work. In the halachic scheme, a teacher, rather than being paid for what he does, is being paid for what he does *not* do. The teacher is thus being paid by society in consideration of his situation and not directly for the service he provides.

Alternatively, since it has been decided that we *can* speak of remuneration for the *melamed*, albeit with a specific point of view, without deviating from the halachah, we might want to inspect the guidelines for remuneration.

Despite the fact that we must pay *sechar batalah*, what a community will pay its teachers is still determined by the amount of significance it ascribes to teaching.

One reason for this is that *sechar batalah* is inestimable, since it is tied to an undefined variable. Just consider: When the teacher is being paid for being suspended from other work, should we assume that the teacher would otherwise have chosen very lucrative work, such as being the CEO of a very large corporation, or that he would have preferred one with more marginal gain? *Sechar batalah* is thus indeterminable. Since this matter cannot really be resolved, payment will be geared to the popular view of *chinuch* in the community. So *sechar batalah* becomes a fine ideal tucked away somewhere in the far reaches of the minds of those who dictate the rates and who pay the salaries of the *melamdim*.

A common scenario might be one where an attorney, sitting on the board of a school, might postulate that it is quite reasonable for a teacher to earn in a week what he himself might charge for a couple of hours of legal services. I do not mean to suggest that all people should earn the same amount — I do not subscribe to a socialist view. I would suggest, though, that respect and consideration must lie at the base of any dealings that involve teachers' salaries.

While it would be inappropriate to aim at making teachers wealthy, it is even less appropriate to aim at keeping a teacher's earnings below the accepted norms.

The same mundane criteria that are generally applied to other kinds of work should govern a *melamed*'s salary — cost of living, average income, local lifestyle. By keeping teachers below a tolerable level of increment we are undermining the entire process of *chinuch*. The field will lack professional appeal and therefore competitiveness. This will in turn deprive a teacher of the respect — and then self-esteem — that are integral to his success.

These observations are more suited to an address to a school board than to a general overview geared to the broad reading audience. It is also important, however, that teachers maintain the right point of view. Although lay persons may frequently lose sight of the *sechar batalah* concept, *mechanchim* never should — at least the spirit of it. In these times of labor unions, contract disputes, and strikes, it is essential that the teacher of Torah bear his identity in mind. While it is in no way wrong for a teacher to desire and vie for security, it is contrary to the spirit of *chinuch* for him to go about actualizing this desire in the same ways as others might. If Jewish children must not be withheld from the study of Torah even for the reconstruction of the Beis HaMikdash, then how could *melamdim* strike to advance salary negotiations without seeking rabbinical dispensation first? (I have seen where, in extreme circumstances, such dispensation was granted.)

So although *chinuch* does not demand that the teacher neglect the day-to-day needs of his own family or that he ignore economic demands, it does demand that he conduct himself according to the dictates of the Torah, and therefore that his bearing should be more noble and exemplary than that of others.

Ethics for the Teacher

IT IS COMMONLY held — and I have reiterated this above — that if a prospective teacher lacks a strong feeling of dedication to teaching, he should seek some other type of work. The *melamed* has been envisioned in Jewish society as one who must have fervor for his work. Some would undoubtedly hold that this is true for any occupation. Whatever you do, be dedicated to it, they would suggest.

While I do not dispute that it is a virtue for any person to be dedicated to his job, I do question the necessity of it. An accountant who feels no particular passion for math may nonetheless be an outstanding accountant. A dentist who fails to feel an ardor for filling cavities is not necessarily considered an inferior dentist. A *melamed*, on the other hand, is entirely unsuited to his endeavor if he feels neither ardor nor passion for what he is doing.

This concept is borne out by various ordinances in halachah, which address a teacher's personal habits. A general proclamation appears in the *Yerushalmi* (*Demai* 7:3): "Regarding a teacher who is lax in his teaching, the verse says, 'Cursed is he who makes the labor of Hashem deceit' " (*Yirmeyahu* 48:10). Thus later authorities state that "we should appoint only teachers who fear God." Rambam (*Hilchos Talmud Torah* 2:3) and the *Shulchan Aruch* (*Yoreh Deah* 245:17) make references to the same verse in *Yirmeyahu* to describe a teacher who leaves the classroom during a session or who spends learning time on other matters.

Obviously a teacher must have a passion for teaching. The aforementioned *Yerushalmi* even says that a teacher must not engage in fasting because it may cause him to be lax in his work. The Rema (*Shulchan Aruch*, loc. cit.) echoes this thought and adds that a teacher must not deprive himself of sleep, even for the purpose of performing the midnight devotions of *tikun chatzos*. All sources agree that a *melamed* should be married, since this will provide his life with stability and peace of mind.

In brief, halachah, besides governing classroom practices, dictates to the teacher the kind of daily life he should lead so that he may maintain his suitability for Hashem's work.

This phenomenon is not predicated on other types of work. While it is virtuous for any person to preserve his health so that he will always be best prepared for his work, the framework of teaching surpasses the realm of native wisdom and common sense and ushers us into the realm of halachah. The rationale is elementary. All of the physical and mental resources of the *melamed* must be in tune with his teaching; it cannot be just a job. (It is probably safe to assume that a *melamed* is dedicated, since one would not be prepared to alter his lifestyle for the sake of a cause to which he is not devoted.) And while it is perhaps possible to mold such devotion in a person — or in oneself — it is preferable that it be present to begin with.

THE BOND BETWEEN teacher and student, if established along the lines of Torah, is unparalleled by any other bond between any two parties. The Maharal's view is that nothing can be as intense. *Tinokos shel beis rabban* are referred to as "God's anointed ones." The reason, according to Abayei, is that they are without sin (*Shabbos* 119b).

The Gemara appears to contradict this: "One should

not teach a student who is not proper" (*Makkos* 10a). Are there then students who are improper? If there are, why did Chazal fail to make the pertinent qualifications in the other passages that deal with *chinuch habanim*?

The answer is that that the *talmid she'eino hagun*, an improper student, is a category that exists only among older disciples and never among *tashbar*. There is no such entity as a young student who is bad as far as Jewish schools are concerned. What the teacher perceives as bad is merely superficial; on a deeper level there is genuine innocence. (The truth is that the issues of so-called bad students or special students are so vital and so complex that they are deserving of the special chapter devoted to it later on.)

The role of the teacher is to address the innocence rather than the surface traits the nonprobing eye sees. Certainly he will also have to deal with surface traits and behaviors, but they are really not the main concern.

The only way for the *melamed* to reach the inner self of the student is to address it with his own inner self. Children, while innocent, are quite astute — often much more than adults — so it is futile for the teacher to make a mere show of trying to communicate with the student. He must be sincere and speak from the heart. A genuine teacher will succeed in relating genuinely to his students.

I am not suggesting that the *melamed* be too self-revealing before his students; excess familiarity can ruin a relationship. But there nevertheless is a particular road to setting up the sought-after bond between rebbe and *talmid*, a bond that incorporates patience, love, and confidence.

Two great teachers of our people described in an identical manner the beauty they sensed in the relationship with their disciples — Rabbi Yehudah HaNassi (see *Makkos* 10a) and a later *Tanna*, Rabbi Chanina (see *Ta'anis* 7a): "I have learned much from my masters, more from my colleagues than from my masters, and more from my students than from all of them." There is in these words a distinct flavor of doing something "with students" rather than "to students." How wonderful for a modern teacher to admit that *he* has learned from his students, that he has gained far more than his students have gained.

Although the Sages have already warned (*Avos* 4:1) that a wise person is one "who learns from every man" — even one lesser than him (see *Bartenura*, loc. cit.) — teachers often feel compelled to present themselves as transcendent beings, incapable of error, omniscient. This compulsion is a product of human weakness, obscures the inner self of a teacher, and casts him in a distorting light. A barrier is thus erected between teacher and student, obstructing the desired encounter between inner selves.

The Gemara and the *Rishonim* have designed a set of principles, which, if followed, pave the way for truly meaningful relationships. A teacher is urged to bolster his image and position, not via the commonly adopted ploys, but rather by following the recipe the Torah provides. There is no doubt that Rabbi Yehudah and Rabbi Chanina conducted themselves according to such principles, and they were as a result able to achieve the most elevated type of bond with their students, a relationship they themselves so aptly described.

IN ANY INTERPERSONAL bond there needs to be a balance between distance and closeness. "The Rabbis learned: Always let the left [hand] push away and the right [hand] draw near" (*Sotah* 47a; *Sanhedrin* 107b). Obviously, if only the former is deployed, the bond will be short-lived. Less obviously, although equally true, excessive closeness also produces a short-lived relationship. An occasional push, then, will solidify a relationship, since it tests it and it can clear the air of previously unresolved feelings and responses. This axiom pertains to all relationships, including the parent-child relationship, and, of course, the teacher-student relationship.

There is, however, a slightly different interpretation of the axiom. When they considered the truths of the human condition, Chazal understood that on occasion a rift may occur in interpersonal relationships. And although we are warned against hating other Jews, we are permitted to feel disconcerted every so often. They thus advised us how to deal with that rift should it happen: "Let the left [hand] push away." If there is cause for rebuke or admonition, let the left hand, that is, the weaker one, do it. "And the right [hand] draw near." When the time for reconciliation is at hand, let the right hand, the stronger one, do it. Chazal recommend that we concentrate our best efforts — the right hand — on improving and enhancing relationships, so that even the occasional rift might be used as a reinforcement.

The same is true for teaching. Frequently a situation will arise that requires a bit of *mussar*, rebuke, or even a punitive measure. When administered, though, it should never be as powerful as the means by which the child will be forgiven and befriended afterward.

A teacher should never bear a grudge against a student. Grudges, in addition to being prohibited by halachah, are juvenile. A teacher should not let a rift linger; rather, he should erase it as soon as possible.

A teacher must be forever cautious never to use punitive measures — especially verbal ones — unless they are warranted *beyond doubt*. If he takes a wrong step, he can rest assured that the child will give undying life to the rift that is formed. As Chazal have taught us, the learning we do as children remains with us forever (that is, unless we reconsider it).

Many will object that punitive measures are never truly necessary. (Curiously, most of these people have little or no experience in the classroom!) Let's take a look at some sources in this matter.

The Midrash states that a father who abstains from reproaching his son contributes to the son's straying toward wrong ways (see *Shemos Rabbah* 21a). Shlomo HaMelech equated the father who "spares the rod" to one who hates his son (*Mishlei* 13:24). Thus, considering that a teacher is considered a father to his students, the same would be held true of a teacher. Also, the Mishnah categorizes the father-son bond together with the teacher-student bond as far as hitting is concerned (see *Makkos* 8a).

The Rambam wrote (*Hilchos Talmud Torah* 2:2) that the "teacher should hit them in order to instill fear in them." He adds, however, that the teacher must avoid "cruelty and hate," and, based on a *gemara* (*Baba Basra* 21a), he states that the teacher is permitted to hit only with a small strap, never with something that might inflict excessive pain. The teacher should hit only in a case of real need, since hitting per se is certainly not virtuous. (The *gemara* in *Makkos* does state clearly, though, that there is a mitzvah to hit occasionally even if the son or student is good in those areas in which the father or teacher wants him to be good.)

It is clear, though, that according to the Torah the teacher has the right to use corporal means of discipline. However, the teacher must never allow the negative reinforcement to be as strong as the positive feeling he should show toward his students. If a teacher can accomplish his pedagogic goals without hitting — or without any negative measures at all — then he certainly should refrain from their use.

It is crucial to add that insults and other forms of verbal abuse are probably far more destructive and counterproductive than old-fashioned corporal punishment. The damage done by bad-mouthing a student is internal and indelible. It has the potency to dampen forever the glow within a young person's heart.

This holds equally true for parents, and even older siblings. A father who treats his child to an ugly assortment of adjectives is possibly being abusive without knowing it. A mother whose high-pitched voice is too commonly a tool of in-house discipline is possibly abusive without intending to be. Parents, however, have a much greater capacity to compensate for this. Educators are far more limited.

It follows, then, that the *melamed* should develop ways to accomplish his goals in a purely positive fashion. But there is a place for punitive measures in the classroom — they can be appropriate in the restricted sense outlined in the halachah.

Alternatively, there is the concept of convention mentioned in halachah. For instance, although women are exempt from the mitzvah of *netilas lulav*, we find that "the daughters of Israel have accustomed themselves to performing that mitzvah." Thus societal convention and common practice can sometimes have an effect on the status of a halachah. Physical punishments appear to be losing their spot within the educational venue. As much as they might be justified by halachah, our schools have adopted the prevalent norms of society on this matter.

There have been abusive teachers, pedagogues who flew off the handle too easily and lost control; there have been educators whose physical punishment of students well exceeded the guidelines of halachah. As a result, corporal punishment of any kind has come to be looked on as unacceptable. The lack of acceptance for such methods today means that, even if according to halachah they are acceptable, they will be destructive of the learning atmosphere — and perhaps your job! Whether or not this is an unfortunate reality, it is nevertheless the case. It is thus highly questionable whether halachah would permit the use of physical punishment today in most school venues, since Jewish society for the most part is so outspoken against it.

IN A SIMILAR vein, the *melamed* should refrain, as much as possible, from raising his voice. In the first place, Shlomo HaMelech warned, "The words of the wise are heard softly" (*Koheles* 9:17). Consistently loud speech was considered by Shlomo HaMelech to be the mark of an imbecile. Second, it creates distance between a teacher and his students. Third, when a teacher demonstrates a loss of composure, he seriously undercuts his own effectiveness. He is less calm, his students become agitated, and learning is threatened. Fourth, a spiral effect comes into play when a teacher establishes a higher volume as the norm, since the students will from then on require that higher level in order to be brought to order.

Also, anger and impatience are inherently poorly suited to a teacher. I am not even referring to real anger; of that Shlomo HaMelech said, "Remove anger from your heart and remove evil from your flesh" (ibid. 11:10). Chazal have taught that anger is one of the most undesirable traits. Rather, I speak of the artificial anger that educators are often so wont to display.

Hillel used to say, "The impatient cannot teach" (*Avos* 2:6). It was this same Hillel who responded patiently and kindly to the impertinent man who requested to be taught the entire Torah while standing on one foot. According to that *gemara* (*Shabbos* 31a), Hillel could not be angered regardless of the provocation. Shammai, on the other hand, Hillel's less patient colleague (or so it seems), when approached by the proselyte asking to be taught the Torah while he stood on one foot, extended to him the courtesy he so richly deserved: Shammai chased him away. The *kapdan*, the strict and impatient teacher, cannot succeed.

The *Shulchan Aruch* (*Yoreh Deah* 246:10), drawing from a Talmudic passage (*Eruvin* 54b), states that "if the master has taught and the students have not understood, he should not be angry with them; he should review and repeat the matter several times until they understand the depths of it...." This, says the Gemara, is the way Moshe taught the people, and this is the way the present-day teacher should teach. Only on one occasion did Moshe express anger with the people, when he said, "Hear, you rebels..." (*Bemidbar* 20:10), and according to some (such as the Rambam) he was punished by the Creator just for this. And that anger was even warranted; it was a reaction to a sin of the people. Anger estranges and impatience inhibits. Neither has any function of a beneficial nature within the pedagogic structure.

This is an area that is traditionally a *nisayon* for parents even more than for teachers. The teacher is hired and paid to be a teacher, and if patience is a necessary feature of his technique, he is obliged to master it. Parents, on the other hand, are not educators for the most part. After Abba has had a stressful day at work (be it *kollel* or business), and after Mom has had a trying day maintaining her home, rearing her younger children, or, as is very often the case these days, working at an outside job, they are sorely lacking patience at the end of the day. Therefore, when they have to spend time reviewing with their children or helping them with homework in the evening, they are in great danger of being angered easily. Thus this imperative cannot be overstated. One must avoid anger at all costs.

ANOTHER GREAT PERIL in putting a single teacher up against a group of students is favoritism, a phenomenon as destructive as it is common. The teacher is wise to bear in mind the drastic results of Yaakov's partiality to Yosef.

The moral teaching derived from that episode is that partiality provokes jealousy, and jealousy brings great disparity in the way people perform.

The common class favorite will almost invariably be the one who excels in his studies. His opposite, the child who seems to accomplish nothing, will be the least favorite, and the unthinking teacher would just as soon do without him altogether. The Sages have warned the teacher against this attitude: "He who learns, learns; and he who does not should not be neglected. He should be placed in a suitable group so that he will learn something" (*Baba Basra* 21a). Destroying the slow achiever's self-confidence is fundamentally equivalent to removing him from the classroom altogether. (Perhaps it is even worse, since he must sit in the class and endure the psychological stress, not to mention his own degradation in the face of his peers.)

Most jealousy is harmful, but there is one area that can generate envy that can be most beneficial — in academic matters among students. The Sages (ibid.) declared that *"kinas sofrim tarbeh chochmah* — academic jealousy increases wisdom." While this adage may have been pronounced with respect to the older scholar, the principle holds true universally. Jealousy, while not a virtue in other areas, is deemed desirable in the arena of learning and spirituality in general.

The teacher is well advised to acknowledge high achievement, but he is wrong to denigrate slow achievers or shame them. Otherwise he is in danger of extinguishing the precious flame burning in the child. He need only remember that the flame burns brightly in every one of them.

THE *MELAMED* SHOULD repeat material several times until everyone understands it. Moshe Rabbeinu made this clear with the words "*Simah b'fihem* — Place it in their mouths" (*Devarim* 31:19). The teacher must ensure not only that the student understands, but that he "possesses" the material, that he has it "in his mouth," capable of repeating it cogently. It would follow that a teacher cannot be satisfied when he hears a *talmid* say the inevitable, "I understand it, but I can't say it over." That cannot be. If the child cannot explain it, then he really does not understand it properly. Perhaps he vaguely comprehends, but that is not good enough. Comprehension, said Moshe, is evidenced only by the student having it "in his own mouth."

Admittedly this accomplishment is not easy to achieve. It is painstaking labor by which even the most minute detail is not to be overlooked. Chances are that if a child fails to grasp a *pasuk* in *Chumash*, for example, what might appear to be a minor facet of the passage is confusing the child and blocking his comprehension. The greatest of medieval commentators, Rashi, devoted vast portions of his work on *Chumash* to the elucidation of various points of grammar, which, if not understood, alter the meaning of many verses drastically. In a sense, Rashi was the prototypal "*Chumash melamed*," showing the modern-day *mechanech* the right path.

It is thus essential that today's students be trained in the technical devices used to examine a text rather than only listening to the complex exegetical monologue of the teacher. Of course, the latter is a type of educational ideal as well, but at a later phase. The former is more primal. It is pointless for a teacher of Torah to digress into a lofty dispute between, say, Kli Yakar and Ohr HaChaim, if the students have not fully mastered the basic elements of the *pasuk* around which that dispute is centered.

The resultant theory of knowledge is basic. A *melamed* must commit the transmission of any material to a series of stages that follow exactly the ordered stages of a child's typical intellectual development into childhood. An infant who begins to pronounce (awkwardly perhaps) his first syllables will gain very little from a lecture on Aristotelian metaphysics, just as an accomplished philosophy scholar would feel silly studying a first-grade reading primer. In both cases the mental effort is poorly matched to the cognitive stage.

Man's cognitive development is what forms the paradigm of all learning. The process commences with the most basic of communication skills — the use of words in isolation — and it culminates (although hopefully it never ends) with a greater degree of abstraction and subtle critical analysis.

Once the child has grasped the word, he can proceed to turn phrases, and before long he can express simple assertive or interrogative statements. Using an inverted pyramid as a metaphor, one can understand the process. In time the scope of word relations broadens and turns more complex as one ascends. The height of thought need not be restricted as long as it is firmly anchored in the basic tools of words and word relations. If this is not so, then all thought is *"osios porchos ba'avir,"* unstable and flighty. It loses touch with reality. The imperative for the *melamed*, then, is to always begin with a technical approach, never to lose sight of the necessary basic skills, and never to proceed until they are mastered.

For the *melamed*, too, his own facility with the primary phases of cognitive development is much more important than scholarship, although scholarship is certainly a desired attribute of the *melamed*. Our *poskim* have cited the ruling of Rabbi Dimi of Neharde'a, who said (*Baba Basra* 21a) that if we must choose between a scholar and a more common person when hiring a *melamed*, we should take the scholar, even if this entails the dismissal of another *melamed*. However, "if there are two *melamdim*, one who has scholarship [and teaches more quantity] but pays little attention to detail, and another who is less of a scholar but pays attention to detail, we should engage the one who teaches with detail."

In the Gemara, Rava argues the side of the scholar by saying that errors of grammar are soon forgotten. Rambam and the *Shulchan Aruch*, however, reject Rava's view and embrace the reasoning of Rabbi Dimi, who felt that once an error of detail enters the mind, it stays put. Attention to detail — spelling, grammar, diction, pronunciation, literal meanings — is apparently of greater significance, certainly with respect to young *talmidim*, than scholarship and covering large portions of material. The reason, as suggested earlier, is that the teacher must be concerned with leading the child's mental faculties through a logical sequence of operations so that comprehension is both solid and broad.

A GREAT THREAT to the efficacy of the teaching process is when a teacher concentrates on his own success rather than on the success of his students. Teaching incorporates the *melamed*'s conveyance of data as well as the students' firm grasp of it. The first of these steps is obviously a necessary prerequisite to the second, but without the second, the first, as a teaching endeavor, is just as meaningless. When a teacher becomes enraptured in the conveyance of data, his oration becomes an art form in his own mind and he fails to realize that he might be speaking to the proverbial walls if his students are not fully comprehending him.

The main goal of education is the students' internalization of what they hear from the teacher. So a teacher who is not so eloquent but is able to accomplish that goal is preferable than his colleague whose oratory skills are outstanding but who is not getting through to his students on *their* level. For a teacher of the second type, the teaching may be little more than an ego trip and will have little or no educational value. Education hinges on communication.

Now let's see what lies at the base of communication. To begin with, when one person seeks to communicate with another, he must first have a clear conception of that other person. This might be the reason, for instance, that some have a difficult time communicating over the telephone. They cannot conceive clearly the party at the other end of the line — his or her frowns, smiles, grimaces, and other facial expressions.

So our attempts at communication depends on our conception of the people with whom we are attempting to communicate, and on our opinion of them, and on who they really are. We would no sooner address royalty with rural colloquialism than we would a child with advanced legalese. The means and methods we use to communicate with people must be matched to *them*. If it is not matched, there is no communication. A teacher, then, must match the means with which he attempts to reach a group of students — young children, teens, boys, girls — to that group. In order to do that, he must first have a clear conception of that group.

This means more than a *maggid shiur* in a yeshivah speaking to his *talmidim* differently from the way an alef-beis *melamed* does in a cheder. It means more than a ninth-grade teacher speaking differently from the way a third-grade teacher speaks. Nor am I referring here merely to speaking. That would be simplistic and needs no restatement.

What I am suggesting is that the *melamed* should probe deeply into the nature of his students and devise means and methods of finding out who they really are. And since it is true that each group is an entity deserving an individualized formulation, we cannot postulate any recipes, since there is an indefinite variety of approaches the *melamed* will have to consider. I have found that each class has its own collective dynamic. That dynamic transcends the separate personalities of the individuals within the class. It seems to exist independently. This dynamic will have ramifications in terms of such areas as academics and behavior. So there is no single formula for all *mechanchim* to follow in building communication.

There is one basic guideline, however, that can be of great service to the teacher. Don't forget that in a student's mind there is a sense that the classroom structure is somewhat contrived. Let's face it. He doesn't view it as the most natural environment, especially in the younger years. A student would prefer some other atmosphere in which he could enjoy the numerous activities of which he can only daydream now. So the more strictly a classroom environment is constructed along the lines of an adult mentality, the more contrived it will appear to a young child and the less comfortable he will feel within it.

In order for the teacher to facilitate communication with his students, he might try to visualize what these students would be doing if they were in an environment of their own choice. Having visualized this, he might try to reconstruct that environment with as many of the trappings as is feasible. He might also want to fashion some of the learning activities after the nonlearning activities that his students would choose to do outside the classroom. They will then come to regard his classroom environment with greater familiarity and contentment. They will feel less alienated within it — or by it. When the entire venue is rendered less of a contrivance in the minds of children, there are greater possibilities for learning.

This applies particularly to children in the primary grades. By the time they have graduated to a higher level, they should feel more at home in the traditional school environment. They will no longer see it as a contrivance, and they will not find it too difficult to learn new subject matter. (Of course, there are many older students who still have difficulties with learning, but that is usually attributable to learning disabilities.) If an older student is more adjusted, it is because he has been ushered into schooling throughout his younger years. Education has become part of him.

This very objective is the ideal of *chinuch* — to make the desire to learn integral to a student's existence. This will be achieved only if the student is instructed and trained in the traditional dynamics of learning. It follows, then, that the child's younger years should involve a gradual but definite induction into those dynamics.

But a contradiction appears to emerge from these two aims. It is recommended that the teacher reconstruct a natural environment for his students inside the classroom, in order to effectively communicate with them; this is realized via a minimization of the traditional learning atmosphere. At the same time, during early schooling a child must be forged into a student by learning and internalizing the processes of education (as distinct from and in addition to the actual content he is learning). How can the teacher achieve both, seemingly opposite goals?

The solution is — as it so often seems to be — balance. Both elements are to be incorporated into the plan. The teacher's immediate goal is communication; without it there can be no learning. The ultimate, and more far-reaching, goal is to train one's students in the ways of schooling. Once the initial goals have been achieved, the teacher should gradually introduce the new modes of learning into the overall process. So the extent to which a *melamed* utilizes singing and playing will decrease at the same rate at which he introduces more complex and more traditional learning procedures.

The underlying objective of it all, though, is the all-important goal of communication.

OUR TORAH IS known as *Toras emes*, the law of truth. This accolade connotes more than the idea that every thought or sentence conforms to logic and reason; it connotes that Torah is *chochmas Elokim*, the wisdom of the Creator. In a sense, Torah is not just true — it is truth itself. The maxims of Torah are the bases for the existence of the universe; the world, modeled after Torah, functions according to it. The Midrash points out that the Almighty "looked into the Torah and created the world" (*Yalkut Shimoni, Bereishis* 2). Elsewhere the Midrash tells us that Torah predated the universe by two millennia (*Bereishis Rabbah* 8:2; *Vayikra Rabbah* 19:1).

The upshot of all this is that one who studies Torah must therefore have a concern for truth. In this vein, the Mishnah teaches us (*Avos* 5:21) that a scholarly dispute that is carried out for the sake of Heaven, where the sincere desire is to ascertain the truth, is praiseworthy and will endure, while a dispute that is not *l'sheim Shamayim* will not endure.

It follows, then, that the pursuit of Torah precludes the aim of achieving self-glorification. Elsewhere the Mishnah states, "Do not make them [that is, the words of Torah] a crown with which to exalt yourself" (*Avos* 4:7). Also, "He who derives personal pleasure from the words of Torah [that is, from the honor bestowed on him because of his scholarship] is removed from the world" (ibid. 1:13, 4:7). The pursuit of Torah must have, at its very foundation, honesty.

The *melamed* finds himself in a position where he might easily overlook this issue of honesty. He is regarded by his students as an authority on Torah, and unless he maintains some sort of control over the development of his own self-image, he may come to regard himself in the same light. Evading introspective thinking will only direct him further toward maintaining this self-image — and sometimes at any cost. One of the costs incurred will be the betrayal of honesty in his transmission of Torah to his students. For example, rather than risk an admission to his students that he does not know the answer to a specific question, he may invent an answer that may satisfy the student but is false.

If the *melamed* continues along this course, he will stray drastically from *Toras emes*. While this might be a peril for any individual who studies Torah, it is worse for the teacher, since he is tempted to present a facade of infallibility before his students. He might even feel, quite mistakenly, that if he does maintain such a facade his students might shun him and that his viability as an educator depends on this.

Honesty in Torah is a theme of considerable primacy in the words of Chazal. Avtalyon warned, "Scholars, give heed to your words, lest you incur the penalty of exile and be banished to a place of evil waters, and the disciples who come after you will drink of them and die, and the Name of Heaven will become profaned" (*Avos* 1:11). "Giving heed to words" means probing Torah with honesty. "Evil waters" refers to distorted thinking and false explanations offered by a rebbe who forfeits honesty. The disciples will drink of these waters and they will "die," which symbolizes a degree of spiritual death, for they will be imbibing a twisted comprehension of the wisdom of the Creator.

It is a great responsibility that obligates the teacher to be cautious — a *talmid*'s partial spiritual death is an ominous price to pay for an unwarranted attempt to save face in the eyes of unsuspecting students.

Besides, the Gemara admonishes, "Teach your tongue to say, 'I do not know,' lest you be caught and trapped in lying" (*Berachos* 4a).

The first dimension of academic dishonesty is that one is causing spiritual damage to his *talmidim*. The second, as the Gemara here illustrates and as was intimated before, is that the teacher might become ensnared in a web of falsehood, a web of his own making.

A third side of the issue has to do with the psychological dynamics of the rebbe-*talmid* relationship. While a disciple is supposed to regard his rebbe as if he were the Almighty (see *Avos* 4:15; *Pesachim* 22b et al.), in reality students do not expect their teacher to know everything. And the student's obvious realization that his teacher is fallible goes together with the teacher's ability to admit that there may be something he does not know. Moreover, and contrary to what a simple-minded teacher might believe, students will sense a contrivance on the part of a teacher who always seems to know everything; they can distinguish between actual knowing and pretend knowing. A teacher's frank admission of not knowing will enhance his students' perception of him as an honest Torah authority and as a genuine human being (assuming, that is, that such admissions do not need to be made too frequently).

Honesty in the study of Torah is transmitted telepathically just as honesty in general is. Dishonesty in Torah also translates into dishonesty overall. Ironically, then, the teacher who uses dishonesty to fortify his own image is in fact defeating his own purpose, because he accomplishes the reverse.

The obligation of the *melamed* is first and foremost to his students, and there is no way to justify presenting them the flimsy fabrications of his mind. He may invent, though, as long as he informs his charges that what he is saying is his own belief or opinion and that it may be incorrect. Rabbi Yishmael said concerning just such a situation, "Do not say, 'Accept *my* view,' for they are allowed [to choose] and not you" (*Avos* 4:10). By coercing students into accepting one's opinion as if it were sacrosanct, one is compromising their dignity.

This brings us to the fourth aspect of academic dishonesty, respect for students, a theme that will be discussed later.

Part Four

GIRLS' EDUCATION

Introduction

Although I look back on more than a quarter of a century as a *mechanech* of girls, I still marvel at the fact that throughout the centuries' long history of *chinuch*, there was never until this century the formal teaching of girls. The events are legendary but bear cursory repetition. Ostensibly these pages will be read by women as well as by men, mothers as well as fathers, *mechanchos* as well as *mechanchim*. Teachers of both genders may find themselves, as I have, teaching young ladies.

There is a special aura that surrounds *chinuch habanos*. What is unique about teaching girls?

The years surrounding World War I found a young Jewish seamstress by the name of Sarah Schenirer establishing the first Bais Yaakov school for girls in the Polish city of Krakow. The name was based on Chazal's explanation that the words *"beis Yaakov"* in the verse *"Ko somru l'beis Yaakov..."* (*Shemos* 19:3) refers to the womenfolk.

At first, many within the Torah community around the world could not fully or easily adjust to this innovation; it appeared to breach the ramparts of Jewish tradition. In truth, it *was* a break with tradition — there was never a Jewish phenomenon of this sort. But it was a necessary one judging from the fresh demands and standards placed before the Jewish family by society as a whole and by new laws passed in the European countries where Jews lived.

Before very long, and with the support of leading Torah luminaries, such as the Gerrer Rebbe, the Imrei Emes *zy"a*, for instance, the Bais Yaakov movement became a dynamic and approved social movement. Within decades hundreds of Bais Yaakov schools (or other similarly inspired institutions under different names) had been established in Europe, the Americas, and Israel, wherein tens of thousands of *talmidos* received formal training — albeit with many variations — in the vast seas of Judaica.

Today, not only is the Bais Yaakov concept no longer regarded as a compromise of Jewish tradition, it seems to portray that tradition in its fullest sense. However, despite the reality of *chinuch habanos*, it is nevertheless a special category within Jewish education. It is one that requires, in many aspects, a unique perspective. In order to develop that perspective, let us analyze several fundamental aspects of the issue:

1. the view of *chinuch habanos* through the eyes of Chazal and halachah,
2. the rationale behind the contemporary movement, and
3. the qualitative difference between teaching Torah to a girl and teaching Torah to a boy.

Chazal and Halachah

There is a dispute among *Tannaim* concerning the Torah education of girls (*Sotah* 20a). Ben Azai held that a father should see to it that his daughter study Torah, while Rabbi Eliezer held that a father must not teach Torah to his daughter because "if one teaches his daughter Torah it is as if he teaches her *tiflus*."

The exact nature of *tiflus* would appear to incorporate a number of improprieties. In its most elemental aspect, it is interpreted as sin, or *devar aveirah*. The Rema states (*Yoreh Deah* 246:6) that teaching a girl Torah is like teaching her to sin. Such a statement requires elucidation, especially in contemporary times when most people would balk at such a thought.

The Gemara later on clarifies, "Torah is the key to wisdom; as soon as Torah enters man, cleverness enters with it" (*Sotah* 21b). Rashi explains that a woman, if equipped with this particular brand of wisdom, will come to trickery and "carry out her desires secretly." There is more than a vague allusion in these words to a woman's particular sort of "desires." Whether this is a social comment of the times or an appraisal of woman's basic nature throughout the ages is difficult to discern from the context itself. Tradition tells us, however, that such statements are definitely deemed to be trans-historical and trans-cultural. So, as difficult as this might be to swallow for many of our contemporaries, Chazal were speaking of womankind throughout the ages. According to Rashi, then, a woman might misuse Torah in a most distasteful way.

Rashi's view, however, need not be regarded as derogatory. He simply held that woman is not suited to the specific activity of learning Torah — for reasons that will surface a bit later — and thus teaching Torah to a woman may result in an abuse of Torah.

Let us consider an analogy to qualify this point. We would surely all agree that sugar is a sweet substance and therefore desirable. At the same time, would we not all agree that if sugar were to get mixed with an entirely incompatible substance that it would cease to be desirable? Still, that fact does not detract from sugar's inherent sweetness. In a similar vein, perhaps Rashi held that there is no more of an innate problem with women than there is with men (nor is there one with Torah), but that the two substances — women and Torah study — are incompatible when mixed. The final product is what is offensive, not the original materials.

(Incidentally, it is interesting to note that Rashi, despite the view cited above, purportedly did teach Torah to his own daughters. They were, in fact, renowned for their erudition in Torah. There is even an opinion that a small portion of Rashi's commentary on *Shas* may have been penned by one of them. Some of the proponents of modernism in Judaism, such as those who wish to see ladies learning Torah alongside men, use Rashi's daughters as one of the bases of their argument. It is not much of an argument, though, considering that Rashi himself did not suggest that females should learn Torah. Whatever the explanation of his daughters' actual studying might have been, it still does not constitute a *hora'ah* for anyone else.)

The view of the Rambam, though it differs slightly from that of Rashi, is the one accepted by the *Shulchan Aruch*. He writes that, in the case of the majority of women, their specific type of intellectual faculty is not oriented toward Torah study. They therefore comprehend Torah in a distorted way, according to their brand of intellect (*Hilchos Talmud Torah* 1:13). The variation from Rashi's view is essentially the omission of the reference to "desire" and "misuse of Torah geared to fulfilling desire." Rambam restricts his words to a purely intellectual consideration. *Tiflus*, according to him, does not mean sin or misuse, but rather gross misunderstanding. There is something undesirable in the distortion of the truths of Torah, so the Rabbis prohibited the teaching of Torah to girls.

Still, just as there may be a distinction between the views of Rashi and Rambam, there is also a significant similarity. Much as Rashi did, the Rambam focused on the outcome of women studying Torah. The result for Rashi was abuse and trickery; for Rambam, distortion. The question that was raised regarding the view of Rashi must also be posed concerning that of the Rambam:

What is it about the nature of woman that disqualifies her from learning Torah? What is it that produces these negative results, whatever they may be?

THE ANSWER TO this question may be rooted in a well-known Talmudic aphorism: "*Nashim da'atan kalos* [or *kalah aleihen*]" (*Shabbos* 33b; *Kiddushin* 80b). Literally translated, this means that the intellect of woman is weak. The significance of this is as follows: The Torah journey is fueled by the workings of the intellect; the sharper the intellect, the better the journey. Woman was not designed by the Creator to fathom the rationalistic depths of the Torah, just as man was not designed to perform the assortment of tasks — physical as well as mental — that are often the exclusive territory of woman.

One need not be a prophet to predict that at least one problem arises out of this understanding. In today's struggle for women's equality and "emancipation," how can we market the idea that woman is less intellectually endowed than man?

There is a second perplexity that arises. There appears to be a contradiction in the words of Chazal. Here we find that they tell us that the *da'as* of woman is weak. Another passage in the Gemara (*Niddah* 45b) finds Rabbi Chisda telling us that the Almighty endowed woman with a *greater* measure of wisdom than He did man — *binah yeseirah*. So while we learn that her *da'as*, intellect, is weaker than that of man, we also learn that her *binah*, wisdom, is greater. What is the difference? And why is there strength or weakness in the specific faculty?

Let's tackle the first question first. It is vital to point

out that we are interested here in the Torah's view of *chinuch* and how it might differ from secular views on education. We have no particular concern for social trends and movements, such as women's liberation. So if there is a difficulty lining up the Torah's timeless teachings with popular opinions of the day, then so be it.

However, I am not saying the words of our Sages were meant to be harmful to the status of woman or denigrating in any way. Anyone who interprets them that way is misunderstanding them.

This is not the right forum for a detailed discussion on the matter of the status of woman within the framework of halachah. Suffice it to say, though, that the issue of equality of men and women per se may be a contrived one to begin with, since the Torah does not concern itself with it, although the Torah does elucidate the essential differences between them. The roles of men and women are distinct in Jewish life, as I suspect they are regarded to be so by mankind as a whole. Distinct, but equally important.

(The sad misunderstanding of this idea on the part of the Western world is probably what gave rise to women's suffrage and liberation movements. In the sphere of the Torah Jew, however, there was never truly a misunderstanding of this. I fear that it was only when the Jew assimilated within non-Jewish culture and adopted the values and attitudes of the society around him that the trouble spilled over into Jewish spheres as well. View it, perhaps, as an imported problem that has no relevance to its new venue.)

The fact that a Jewish woman is not obligated to

wear tefillin, for instance, is not indicative of her inferiority, just as the fact that a man is unable to bring human life into this world is not indicative of his inferiority. The Almighty created the two species *zachar u'nekeivah* — male and female — with the intention that together, in unison and with equality (but *not* redundantly), they would form the beauty and wholeness of human life. So, without ever alluding to the notion of inequality, Chazal merely uncovered the innate attributes that distinguish men from women. After all, didn't Rabbi Akiva proclaim to his thousands of disciples that all of his Torah knowledge, as well as theirs, were the "possession," that is, to the credit and merit, of his illustrious wife, Rachel? How does inequality fit into that paradigm?

Thus, here, too, when they deal with the topic of intellect and its various functions and faculties, the Sages are not making a statement about woman's inferiority or man's inferiority when they describe the particular strengths of each — *da'as* in one case and *binah* in the other.

Ultimately, then, the key to understanding the issue lies with an analysis of the two concepts, *da'as* and *binah*, and an attempt to decipher why each gender has been empowered in its specific way.

BASED ON THE words of Chazal in many places, *da'as* corresponds to the human faculty of grasping the abstract and strictly logical truths, while *binah* refers to intuitive and experiential knowledge. With his stronger measure of *da'as* man is more attuned to comprehending truths that have a rational underpinning. With her heightened *binah*, woman has the greater ability to perceive that which is concealed from the eye and is not necessarily derived from reason and logic. Both *da'as* and *binah* are tools of a very specific nature, utensils the Creator granted to men and women so they may deal with the world around them in the manner most suited to them. In His infinite wisdom, He assigned *da'as* to man, although certainly not at the total exclusion of women, and He bestowed *binah* on woman, although not at the total exclusion of this faculty to man. (It is interesting to note that in the *sefiros* that Chazal offer us, the hierarchy of the dimensions of penetrating reality according to Kabbalah, *binah* is on a higher rung than *da'as*.) These are descriptions, then, of the essences of men and women that Hashem created.

Obviously the Torah assigns tasks to people according to their essence. Torah study, an endeavor that aspires to truth, requires the particular faculty of *da'as*. Woman, not properly empowered in the required faculty, is thus not attuned to this task. If she would attempt to perform this task, the result would be *tiflus* (according to Rashi's interpretation, Rambam's, or both). Hence Chazal decided that it would be best for women not to learn Torah.

WHAT IS MOST crucial, though, is that we know that women do have meaningful openings to the chambers of Torah. One of the Mishnah's views cited earlier, that of Ben Azai, was that a father *is* obligated to teach Torah to his daughter. Within the context of that *mishnah*, Ben Azai explains his opinion: if the girl in later years might be required, *chas v'shalom*, to drink the waters of the *sotah*, she must be learned enough to comprehend what is involved.

It is curious that Ben Azai felt that a girl should study Torah only because of the possibility of a certain predicament, a possibility that is tremendously remote (not to mention the fact that the particular predicament would be indicative of anything *but* a woman who has Torah at heart).

Furthermore, if this really is the sole or primary aim of girls' *chinuch*, then, today, in the post–Beis HaMikdash era, when the *sotah* waters are no longer administered, would Ben Azai declare that there is no point in providing Torah education for Jewish girls?

It appears, by virtue of later *poskim*, who grappled with Ben Azai's opinion, that he was actually not concerned with the waters of the *sotah* but with *any* circumstances in which she would have to have a background in Torah knowledge. The aim of girls' learning, in the view of Ben Azai, is that a woman needs to be knowledgeable so that she will be able to perform her halachic duties with an understanding of what she is supposed to do.

Tosafos (*Sotah* 21b), however, took Ben Azai as meaning even more than this: girls should learn in the same type of framework as boys, because there is a commandment that girls learn Torah. They cite a passage from the *Yerushalmi* that draws a distinction between the opinion of Ben Azai and the opinion of Rabbi Elazar ben Azariah, who held the following:

> The Torah commands, "Congregate the nation — the men and the women and the children and the

strangers who are inside your gates — in order that they shall hear, and in order that they shall learn, and they will fear God" (*Devarim* 31:12). The men came to learn, and the women came to hear.

(Chagigah 3a)

Tosafos explains that the last phrase in the verse is telling us that it is actually a mitzvah for women to hear, but for extrinsic reasons, that is, in order that they should know how to perform the mitzvos. The objective notwithstanding, it *is* a mitzvah! It was Rabbi Elazar ben Azariah who advised that a woman should study Torah with the practical aim of Torah observance. Ben Azai, *Tosafos* maintains, merely added that a girl should learn for the sake of learning itself, for she is commanded to do so. (But with or without the view of Ben Azai, a woman is obligated to study Torah, although perhaps not all of the Torah.)

This conclusion is strengthened by a second *Tosafos* (*Chagigah* 3a), which cites the same *Yerushalmi* and summed up Ben Azai's opinion simply: "A man must teach his daughter Torah." This source omits Ben Azai's reasoning quoted in the Mishnah and stresses only the fact that a father has the obligation of teaching Torah to his daughter. And it is clear that the obligation is for the sake of learning itself.

I suppose it is possible to surmise that Ben Azai assessed woman's nature differently from the others. If his dictum were accepted, *chinuch* for girls would have run concurrently with *chinuch* for boys throughout the centuries. His view was rejected, however, at least as far as practice is concerned. There is no question, then, that men alone are bound by the commandment of *talmud Torah*, study for its own sake.

Rabbi Elazar ben Azariah's observation is vital, though. Jewish women have a world of Torah observance at which they must be proficient; how can they possibly achieve this without a familiarity with at least the practical dynamics of halachah? And how can a Jewish woman summon the right *kavanos* (intentions and devotions) if she is not learned in the underlying principles of halachah? So, at the very least, girls must be taught halachah.

Alternatively, neither the Rambam nor the *Shulchan Aruch* made mention of this concept. This might be because it is so obvious. The Rema, however, in his glosses to the *Shulchan Aruch* (*Yoreh Deah* 246:6), does state this clearly: "Women must learn those laws that pertain to women." This, then, concludes the first opening through which woman enters the realm of Torah study.

THERE IS A second. Both Rambam and the *Shulchan Aruch* declare that a woman who does go ahead and study Torah will receive Heavenly reward, although not as great as the reward that will be given to a man, who was commanded in the mitzvah of Torah study. This is a principle that affects countless areas. If someone is not actually commanded to perform a divine commandment but does it anyway, he is praiseworthy, although less so than the person who *is* commanded to do the act and does it (*Avodah Zarah* 3a; see also *Tosafos*, loc. cit.; s.v. "*gadol hametzuveh v'oseh...*")

So in general the father, or the community as a

whole, is not obligated to initiate Torah study for girls. Moreover, the father is halachically prohibited from teaching Torah to his daughter, as we have seen. But a woman may, of her own initiative, study Torah, even without the blessings and sanction of a formal institution. On the contrary, the fact that a woman can receive reward for studying Torah signifies that she is doing something worthwhile.

Alternatively, since tradition has established and maintained restrictions limiting women's Torah study, it behooves the individual to embrace the tradition rather than ignore it.

A THIRD OPENING, small though it may be, also exists. The prohibition for a father to teach his daughter Torah applies only to *Torah shebe'al peh* — Mishnah, Gemara, and related commentaries — according to both Rambam and *Shulchan Aruch*. It is the oral tradition that a father should not teach his daughter, or it is as if he is teaching her *tiflus*. Regarding *Torah shebiksav*, however, the prohibition appears to be no more than a recommendation and not something truly binding. Therefore, as they state, if a father teaches his daughter the written law, it is *not* as if he taught her *tiflus*.

There is another opening through which women enter the hallowed chambers of Torah, the opening that is possibly the most essential one. It comes by way of a halachah cited in *Shulchan Aruch* (*Orach Chaim* 47) to the effect that women are obligated to recite *birkos haTorah*, the blessings recited over Torah study each morning, just as their male counterparts do.

What is the underlying reason for this? Both the Magen Avraham and the Turei Zahav explain that there are two factors. First, the blessings are in place of the sacrifice of the *tamid shel shachar*, the daily offering brought in the morning, which was offered for the benefit of the entire people, including the women. Second, women, as was noted earlier, are obligated to learn the halachos that pertain to them and are therefore included in the obligation of Torah study.

Another element deserves mention in this context, though. The text of the first of the blessings is "*v'tzivanu la'asok b'divrei Torah.*" The key term is the infinitive *la'asok*, which renders the translation as "to be involved with the words of Torah." There is no mention of the notion that we were commanded to *study* Torah, only the fact that we were commanded to be *involved* with the words of Torah.

What is the nature of involvement? Clearly an involvement is much more of a pervasive concept than learning. *La'asok* denotes a preoccupation and an overall orientation and way of thinking. And there can be no doubt that women are as obligated to develop and adopt a pervasive Torah outlook as much as Jewish men — if not more so. The resultant claim would be that anything that will promote a Jewish woman's obtaining the correct Jewish orientation ought to be pursued, for it will facilitate her fulfillment of her obligation.

BASED ON ALL this, we can make the following halachic conclusions:
1. Girls should be taught the practical aspects of Torah, such as halachah.

2. Girls may study Torah on their own initiative, if they so desire, although traditionally they do not.

3. There is no absolute prohibition against teaching the Written Torah to girls.

4. There is a clear prohibition against teaching girls the oral tradition. (This refers to works other than practical halachah, works of *hashkafah*, *mussar*, and Midrash, which are ostensibly commentaries of the Written Torah, not essentially unlike the commentaries of Rashi and Ramban.)

Let us now turn our analysis to the sudden interest in the field and why the Bais Yaakov movement has swept the entire Jewish world.

The Contemporary Movement

In the realm of halachah there is a unique category known as *hora'as sha'ah*, which refers to a special rabbinical dispensation and urgent ruling (*Pesachim* 82b; *Yoma* 69b; *Yevamos* 35 et al.). A famous example of *hora'as sha'ah* is when Eliyahu performed a sacrifice on an altar on Mount Carmel in spite of the prohibition against *bamos*, altars outside the Mikdash (see *Melachim* I, ch. 18). The momentary but urgent need to deal effectively with the priests of Baal and to thereby guide *klal Yisrael* was stronger in Eliyahu's estimation than the prohibition of *bamos*. Therefore he ruled that a sacrifice should be offered. This was a *hora'as sha'ah*. That Eliyahu's decision received approbation from Above is evident from the account that ensued.

Situations can arise that present threatening ramifications. Our rabbis are empowered by Torah to deal with such situations in an apropos manner, even if that entails an alteration or even a reversal of a previous halachic decision. But part of what is fundamental to the notion of *hora'as sha'ah* is that it does not necessarily serve as a precedent for the future. It is restricted in application only to the state of affairs it was dispensed to deal with. In other words, only as long as the threatening situation lingers can the ruling of the *hora'as sha'ah* continue to be applied.

I feel it is reasonable to suggest that the rabbinical sanction for girls' Torah study in our era can be ascribed to this notion of *hora'as sha'ah*. The deliberations leading up to the ultimate approval revolved around a dramatically perilous new situation. It was not due to a sudden belief in the principle of *chinuch habanos* that Bais Yaakov received communal assent; it was rather due to a keen appreciation of a fresh set of circumstances that presented a colossal threat to the future of the Jewish people.

WITH THE ADVENT of the modern world came so-called enlightenment — broadened communications, social upheaval, varied learning. These phenomena, while often deemed by the nations of the world as being for the betterment of the human condition, also entailed moral decay and changing value systems. It comes as no surprise, then, that all this immensely facilitated the destructive tide of assimilation. Neither was it surprising that countless Jewish youths, who grew up witnessing the persecution and poverty of their people in Eastern Europe, suddenly latched on to new ideological trends in the hope of overcoming what they predicted would be a similar lot in life for themselves. Their counterparts in central and western Europe had long since tasted the delicacies of acculturation and freedom from Torah's law.

These tendencies began, with increasing speed, to breach the heretofore impenetrable fortifications of the Eastern European Jewish home. And with such devastating force did it occur that hundreds of thousands of Jewish souls became lost to Torah. That deluge, had it remained unchecked, would have gnawed away at the very foundations of the nation, until the Jewish people's future would have been imperiled.

The danger was considered even more potent with respect to girls. Young Jewish men could still be protected by the walls of the *beis midrash* and by the isolation of the yeshivah. Sure, young men fell victim to the new wave, but there was still something of a structure that could hold them.

Matters were different for young Jewish women. While the home had many centuries earlier ceased to be the lone beacon of light for Jewish boys, for their sisters the home remained the sole teacher and guide. But society's new laws were dragging Jewish girls out of the house to attend public schools, where they came into contact with various people, arts, sciences, beliefs, and influences. And the new ideological waves were making themselves felt more and more.

So as the sanctity and the solidarity of the home were endangered, it was particularly Jewish girls who were at risk. Whereas once they had learned the faith and the customs of their nation in the confines of the family, they now started a search for new "truths" beyond the shelter of the home. They would now look for "relevance" (if I may borrow a more contemporary expression) at poetry recitals, at political rallies, at secular Zionist meetings. Unprepared as they were for this sudden exposure, their reactions tended to be extreme, resulting in a denial of *Yiddishkeit*. Young Jewish womanhood was being shaken to its roots.

THE TRAGEDY IN all this was the lure of assimilation. This was partially attributed to the fact that for young women there was a lack of an equal attraction within the system of Torah. Some reasoned that if young Jewish women were presented with invigorating social challenges and learning experiences *within* the system, they would probably have pursued them rather than stray from tradition. Most would have been satisfied, it was argued, to derive their "relevance" from Torah in much the same way as their brothers who attended yeshivos.

But there was nothing to be gained from bemoaning the past while the present and future were open to rectification. Thus a sense of divine purpose was born in the mind of a young woman from Krakow. In short order the notion of *chinuch habanos* spread dramatically, filling the void young Jewish women were feeling.

The benefits were both immediate and far-reaching. The immediate benefit was that the winds of assimilation were substantially blocked and a generation of Jewish girls were kept within the fold. The far-reaching effect was of greater significance: the very fiber and spirit of *klal Yisrael* has been preserved as a result of Bais Yaakov. And now, with the speedy moral deterioration of today's clime, the role it plays is all the more vital.

In addition, the vitality of the Jewish people is maintained through its Torah. In our day this is contingent on the *kollel*, whereby young married men can devote themselves to Torah study while their wives exert themselves in the maintenance of the family. The required *mesirus nefesh*, self-sacrifice, for the Jewish woman to do this is, at least in the contemporary world, a direct product of the successful teachings of the Bais Yaakov experience.

Hence the preservation of a people!

Chinuch HaBanos: A Qualitative Definition

We cited earlier a Talmudic dictum to the effect that woman has greater wisdom than man. The Hebrew word for wisdom, *binah*, is linguistically connected to the Hebrew word for construction, *binyan*, according to the Midrash (*Bereishis Rabbah* 18:1). In fact, the verse from which Chazal derive woman's abundant wisdom is "*Vayiven es hatzeila...* — [The Almighty] built the rib that He had taken from the man into a woman" (*Bereishis* 2:22). This implies that it is precisely woman's characteristic of *binah* that enables her — and compels her — to be the builder of the Jewish home.

Based on this, Chazal point out, for instance, that "*beiso zu ishto*," one's home is a reference to one's wife (first *mishnah* in *Yoma*). Often we ascribe the essence of a building to its architect. Therefore, woman, who constructs the Jewish home and maintains the family unit, is symbolic of the Jewish home itself. This is due to her ability to build, a function of her *binah*.

This touches on the true calling of Jewish women according to the Torah: the building and preservation of the Jewish home. (This is not necessarily a reference to physical maintenance of the household, but rather more to the esoteric aspects.) The presence of the woman in the home is what imbues its atmosphere with its wholesomeness. This is what is so vital to the husband's — and the sons' and daughters' — success as Torah Jews, even as *menschen*. In reality, then, the Torah of Jewish men is a direct consequence and beneficiary of the women's efforts. Though there are numerous allusions to this, I will cite only three.

THE FIRST IS a verse that must be exhausted from being quoted so often with respect to girls' Torah learning. And though I can offer my apologies to the reader for citing it yet again, I feel that this verse offers the most fundamental understanding of the topic.

The Almighty said to Moshe, "Thus shall you say to the house of Yaakov, and you shall speak to the children of Israel" (*Shemos* 19:3). A comment of the *Mechilta* explains that the "house of Yaakov" refers to the women, while the "children of Israel" refers to the men.

The divine message Moshe was supposed to convey to them was "You shall be for Me a kingdom of priests and a holy nation" (ibid., 6). The first point one notices is that it was essential that Moshe address these words not only to the men, but also to the women. That would be a crucial part of his bid to urge the people toward priestliness and holiness.

It is also most curious that the Almighty mentioned

the house of Yaakov before the children of Israel. Perhaps the intention was that there is even greater significance in telling the women than there would be in telling the men. It is not surprising, then, that we find just this thought expressed in the commentary of the Maharsha (see his glosses to *Sotah* 21a). He explains: In the second half of the Almighty's command to Moshe, He says, "And you shall speak [*v'sageid*] to the children of Israel." Grammatically the verbal conjugation in the future tense for second-person singular masculine (*atah*) is identical to the conjugation for third-person singular feminine (*hi*). Thus the command "*v'sageid*" can also mean, "*she* shall speak." Thus we can read the verse, "Thus shall you speak to the house of Yaakov [the women], and *she* shall speak to the children of Israel [the men]."

The upshot of the Maharsha's interpretation is that Moshe was to relay these urgent words only to the women, and it would be they who would transmit the message to their husbands. Perhaps because this way it could be done with greater impact than if Moshe would speak to the men himself. The women of the nation would see to it that the husbands, sons, and brothers would internalize the call for sanctity as a true ideal. The reason is woman's capacity to build, to plant commitment to Torah, even where none existed before (as in the case of Rabbi Akiva's wife).

The second allusion is a quote from *Mishlei*: "Listen, my son, to the rebuke of your father, and do not forsake the Torah of your mother" (*Mishlei* 1:8). Shlomo HaMelech is telling us that the lessons and instructions of a father and mother should be the guides that lead a man through life. The father's words are referred to as *"mussar,"* rebuke, while the mother's lessons are labeled "Torah." In explaining why this distinction exists, both Ibn Ezra and Ralbag point out that it is the mother, more than the father, who shows her son the right path and leads him along it.

For the third source, we turn to a well-known passage from the Gemara (*Berachos* 17a), where the woman is accredited not only with being a righteous role model for her family, but also with facilitating the pursuit of Torah by the male members of her family. "What is the merit of women?" asks the Gemara. "That she escorts her sons to the *beis rabban* and that she encourages her husband to go to the house of study and awaits his return."

Clearly, whereas man's life's mission is the actual study of Torah, woman's life's mission is laying the foundation — establishing and maintaining the inner force and commitment necessary for it. The Torah of the family is ascribed to the efforts of the woman who heads that family. So unquestionably the woman is a full partner in the Jewish experience of the family unit. It is she who portrays the best of qualities herself and who instills the same in her husband and son. And it must be she who personifies a commitment to Torah and who will instill the same in her husband and son. Little wonder that the Almighty revealed this timeless truth to Moshe. The key to the hearts and souls of the Jewish people was in the hands of the nation's women.

GETTING BACK TO our original subject — the far-reaching objective of the Bais Yaakov movement — it is evident that the adherence of the people to the laws and values of *Yiddishkeit* lay (and lies) in the hands of the Jewish woman. The challenges the Eastern European Jewish girls faced at the turn of the century were forerunners to the greater dangers to the spiritual security of an entire nation. The Bais Yaakov movement provided, through its graduates, a new and fortified resource of Jewish womanhood, appropriate wives and mothers for the coming generations. The young *mechaneches* would be capable of taking the reins of leadership and safeguarding the viability of Jewish society according to Torah.

Based on all this, we can now list several pedagogic imperatives for the enterprise of *chinuch habanos*:

1. As vital as girls' Jewish education obviously is, it is distinguished from boys' learning in that it is not necessitated by any of the 613 divine commandments. It is *not* part of the overall mitzvah of *talmud Torah*. The education of girls, then, should not be aimed at instilling that sense of obligation to study Torah. Therefore, for example, whereas the halachah teaches us that a boy should learn Torah during part of the night, this does not apply to girls. Similarly, any of the numerous specific regulations that affect boys' learning likely do not pertain to *chinuch habanos*.

2. A significant portion of time spent in teaching Torah to girls must be devoted to the study of halachah. Since a primary aim in teaching Torah to girls is to prepare them for practical Judaism, halachah is a major goal. It goes without saying

that boys must learn halachah as well, since "study leads to action," as the Gemara states (*Kiddushin* 40b). Still, in the traditional yeshivah program only a small percentage of study time is devoted to it. Girls' learning is thus vitally different in this regard.

3. Girls' study of sacred texts, apart from practical works of halachah, must be restricted to Tanach and its commentaries and to works of ethics and *mussar*. The overall message of the authorities is that girls may not delve into *Torah shebe'al peh*. The only segments of the oral tradition that would be permissible would be those that fall into the categories listed. Therefore *Pirkei Avos* and the *aggadah* sections in the works of Chazal (such as *midrashim*) would be acceptable studies for girls.

4. The comprehensive category known as *hashkafah Yehudis*, Jewish philosophy, is a crucial element in the learning menu of young Jewish women. It is comprised of the themes and particulars of Jewish "feeling" — toward the Almighty, man, and the world. History, and anything else of a broad nature addressing Jewishness, would fall into this category.

5. One of the most controversial areas emanating from a discussion of *chinuch habanos* is mixed classes. Beyond the halachic difficulties involved in having boys and girls mingle in this (or any other) venue, the standpoint of pure pedagogy precludes it. We have discovered that there are qualitative distinctions between the learning of

boys and that of girls. If education is so gender specific, how can both groups be taught in the same venue at the same time? Separation is thus an imperative. At exactly which age this separation should be enforced is subject to some degree of interpretation. Traditionally separation begins at the earliest stage, although some feel that for the preschool years there is no reason to implement it.

Despite the many distinctions between the guidelines for teaching boys and those for teaching girls, I believe I am fully justified in claiming that educators involved in *chinuch habanos* should sense the same sense of mission and purpose as their colleagues who teach boys. This is especially true today, when society holds forth dangers that are as grave as any throughout the history of our people. The *mechanchim* of today's Jewish women are in large measure the *mechanchim* of generations — of Jews who live well beyond their classrooms and their time.

Part Five

GENERAL STUDIES IN THE YESHIVAH

Introduction

During the grand old days when I was in yeshivah, my friends and I would sometimes sit and shmooze about what lay in store for us. There were those who had it all planned out. They would leave the hallowed halls of the yeshivah world and pursue a profession. Some of them are, in fact, accountants, attorneys, and physicians today. Many eventually wound up in the business world (and their fortunes vary today as much as one might imagine), although that was not specifically part of the plan.

Then there were those of us who considered ourselves the elite, those for whom a life of Torah and lofty academic pursuits was greater than anything that could possibly be conceived.

But what about *parnasah*? At first the very term carried with it a sense of loathing; it was something we considered beneath ourselves to even be concerned about. That will take care of itself somehow, we knew.

I tended to be a bit more practical, so I reasoned that after some years in *kollel* I would perhaps enter the field of *rabbanus* (something the *rosh yeshivah* whom I quoted in an earlier chapter actually tried to persuade me to do). Or I would become an "outreach professional," an occupation that was very close to my young heart. Or I would go into *chinuch*!

However, if anyone had come up with the ludicrous suggestion that I would end up having any sort of connection with the world of general studies in the yeshivah system, I would have scoffed, perhaps even been insulted. That was as remote from my thinking as the quest for a profession. I would devote my life to Torah, in one form or another, and teaching English, quite frankly, did not fit into that scenario.

Funny, though, how a person entertains certain notions and the *Ribbono shel Olam* entertains others. Who would have believed back then that general studies would end up comprising a fair portion of my educational career? Things just worked out that way. *Parnasah* demands made themselves felt with increasing urgency, and the opportunity arose. So I asked the Torah luminaries whose words had provided me with guidance at virtually every major juncture, and I accepted an offer to teach English and history at the high-school and junior-high levels.

The rest is history (pardon the pun!). As I write these lines I figure I have spent the past twenty-three years involved substantially in general studies in addition to *limudei kodesh*. I have also enjoyed the position of general studies principal for the last fifteen of those. Over that time I developed a view of general studies that I think is worth sharing.

Introduction

Limudei chol remains, to my thinking, one of the most interesting (both colorful as well as complex) aspects of *chinuch* and the one that is in need of a proper philosophical position more than any other. So let's take a look at the following themes having to do with general studies (henceforth to be referred to as GS):

1. What is the underlying difference between teaching *kodesh* and teaching *chol*?
2. Does GS really have a part in the life of a yeshivah student?
3. Why would any young *chinuch* hopeful consider GS as part of his or her career options?

Kodesh versus Chol

The word *ohel*, tent, is used in several instances in the Torah to denote the concept of Jewish learning. Yaakov was a *"yosheiv ohalim"* (*Bereishis* 25:27), which means that he spent his life immersed in the study of Torah. Also, "This is the law [Torah]: If a man dies in a tent..." (*Bemidbar* 19:14). Chazal have interpreted this verse as indicating that one cannot hope for his Torah knowledge to endure unless he "kills himself for it," unless he "dies in the tent of Torah" (*Berachos* 63b). Consider also the verse "Rejoice, Zevulun, in your going out and Yissachar in your tents" (*Devarim* 33:18). The Midrash relates that the two brothers arranged a partnership between themselves — Zevulun would "go out" and engage in business, from whose profits he would support Yissachar, who would remain "in the tent," studying Torah.

Why is the tent an appropriate symbol? It is because *ohel* indicates a certain atmosphere. The tent is not merely a dwelling place; it is a structure that completely envelops anything or anyone that is inside it, more so than other structures. Thus the notion of *tumas ohel*, the ritual impurity that descends upon anything that is inside the same enclosure as a corpse. Although the same law applies to a house as much as to a tent, the *tumah* is referred to as *tumas ohel* because *ohel* is a designation for an atmosphere that affects all that is inside it. The same applies to things that are *tahor*, ritually pure. Thus, when an object enters a tent, it does not just undergo a change in location; it experiences a dramatic shift that touches upon values and spirit.

When Avraham was asked by the three angels the whereabouts of his wife, Sarah (*Bereishis* 18:9), he responded that she was "in the tent." Chazal drew a message from this brief response, that Sarah portrayed the attribute of modesty fundamental to Jewish womanhood (*Yevamos* 77a). If this was a response to the angels' question, though, we must infer that the angels were not asking about the geographical location of Sarah, but rather about her nature, about the spirit she infused into her home. Thus Avraham answered with a reference to her nature, satisfying the angels that Sarah was most suited to being the pillar of the Jewish family, the Jewish nation.

How? She was "in the tent." She was the architect of a pervasive atmosphere. She was herself wholly immersed in those environs, so she was able to maintain them.

In a similar sense, Torah study requires a complete immersion in a certain atmosphere. It is thus inappropriate to approach the topic of Torah study in the same way one approaches any other type of learning. Torah is "your life and the length of your days" (*Devarim* 30:20). The essence of Torah study is that it leads to practice (*Kiddushin* 40b). It therefore also hinges on real involvement.

Rabbi Chanina ben Dosa said, "He whose wisdom exceeds his deeds, his wisdom does not endure" (*Avos* 3:13). The Maharal (*Nesiv HaTorah*, ch. 1) explained the reason for this. Torah study is a transcendent intellectual endeavor. If it is not actualized by the performance of physical acts, it escapes the one who has engaged in it, for it cannot be maintained in this world other than through actualization. The very term *Torah* denotes "showing the way," that is, teaching about actual life and how we ought to live it.

That is why the study of Torah is carried on in an *ohel* — all aspects of life hinge on it. With this groundwork, we can fully understand the differences between *kodesh* and *chol*.

THE FIRST DIFFERENCE, which we have already touched on, is atmosphere. It is more far-reaching than I have intimated. Even in secular education there is talk of "school atmosphere." For us, atmosphere in *chinuch* is different. It is universal and it is trans-historical. For example, the *Shulchan Aruch* (*Yoreh Deah* 245:5) states that a child should in his early years study the book of *Vayikra*. In this way he will commence his Torah studies with the laws of purity. Although there are many fine schools that do not adhere to this halachah, the regulation was intended for all Torah schools everywhere in the world.

Thus any two children who study Torah anywhere

immediately have common ground. The *Shulchan Aruch* is the same for both, so the way they bring their Torah into actuality is the same. Thus the location of the two particular schools is insignificant. Now that's atmosphere!

GS, on the other hand, need not contribute to the atmosphere of *chinuch*. And while certainly they should not detract from the atmosphere, they are not principal elements of it.

ANY LEARNING INSTITUTION anywhere, whether it teaches the writings of Aristotle or the techniques of guerrilla warfare, professes to teach only that which is worthwhile. Obviously. If it is not worthwhile, why teach it? Still, it is universally held that there is a distinction between things that are intrinsically valuable and those that are extrinsically valuable. The type of learning that has intrinsic value is the sort that is carried on for its own sake, and it is not aimed necessarily at producing anything beyond itself. A study that has extrinsic value, though, is one that is geared at providing a skill or ability beyond the study itself. It is learned for some purpose, and it is therefore not by definition good in its own right.

All would agree that subjects such as math, physics, and composition hold possible "keys for the future," since a great many vocational fields require these skills. They are therefore of extrinsic value. While some would argue that any knowledge can be pursued for its own sake, I would contend that this is not the way people view the matter. Thus math becomes applied math, and physics becomes applied physics.

To prove the point, let's consider how often teachers of GS are asked by many a disgruntled student, "Why do we have to learn this stuff?" In the case of math and composition or other such subjects, the teacher should have an easy time describing the myriad uses for these skills later in life. But when it comes to French and poetry or some social studies, it is not quite as easy. But not too many teachers today would answer that these nonskill subjects are to be pursued for their own sakes. They might pontificate about the legacies of Western culture or the preservation of a society's heritage, but even those are not intrinsically valuable concerns from a philosophical standpoint. So intrinsic value seems to be something of which most, if not all of, GS is patently devoid.

In this respect, *limudei kodesh* is very different. Torah is learned because of what it is — *chochmas Elokim* — and not for what it produces. And although, as we noted, the greatness of Torah is that it leads to practice, we must not forget the *mishnah* that declares, "*Talmud Torah kenegged kulam* — The study of Torah is greater than all the other commandments together" (*Peah* 1:1).*

The Rambam tells us (*Hilchos Talmud Torah* 3:4) in the name of the Gemara that if one must choose between doing a mitzvah and learning Torah, he should learn, provided that the mitzvah will be performed by another.

Hashem warned Yehoshua, "Never shall this book of

---

* Some explain that even that is a result of Torah study leading to action, but Rav Shamshon of Shantz quotes a *Yerushalmi* that says that the meaning of the *mishnah* is that the total of all the mitzvos is not as *precious* as one letter of Torah.

Torah be removed from your mouth" (*Yehoshua* 1:8). The Jews must always be occupied with Torah. Clearly this suggests a study for intrinsic value. Certain segments of Torah, such as halachah, do teach skills in a broad sense, but students of Torah spend far more time learning the segments that do not. The only reason a Jew is compelled to learn and teach Torah is that he believes it to be "the highest order of knowledge." It would be rare for a *talmid* to ask, "Why do we have to learn this?" with regard to Torah. The child understands that Torah knowledge is intrinsically important, unless, that is, the child is somewhat rebellious (in which case a special approach needs to be taken).

Does this mean that within the framework of Torah there is no concern for any practical purposes? Are the keys to the future to be neglected in our system? Well, *chinuch*, in and of itself, is separate from such considerations, but it certainly does not exclude them.

Well known is the *mishnah* (*Kiddushin* 29a) that tells us that a father is obliged to teach his son "Torah and a craft." The halachah is conscious of vocational prerequisites — it admonishes the father that he should not forget them. Note, however, that Torah and a "craft" are separate. So it very well may be appropriate that a Torah school also impart skills that will help in securing a livelihood later on, but those skills are not strictly part of the Torah learning of the child — they are in addition to it.

As important as they are, then, GS skills and other studies are at best extrinsically valuable, while Torah has intrinsic value. This is a crucial distinction.

WHEN IS AN undertaking considered successful? What constitutes success? There is no doubt that when an undertaking has a specific aim, success will be actual when that goal has been realized. The successes of *limudei kodesh* and *limudei chol* are by no means the same, since the two enterprises have objectives that are quite distinct.

Etymologically the term *education*, which is derived from the Latin infinitive *duco* and prefix *e*, means "drawing out." Once the learning has been drawn out of the inner reservoir of the student, he is considered educated. "Is that man educated?" one might ask. The response will depend entirely on the standard by which a person in society is called educated. If a sixth-grade diploma is the minimum, then that man will be educated if he has it. If a doctorate is required, then he will be educated if he has that. Whatever the accepted norm will be, a person's right to be called educated will depend on whether he has lived up to it. And it is possible to live up to that goal and to achieve that standard. So success in education, and therefore in GS, entails the completion of a specific process.

This is not at all true when it comes to *chinuch* and to *limudei kodesh*. It is not that there can be no success. It is simply that success is measured in an opposite fashion. Let's examine some nomenclature in order to discover the underlying thought.

With us Jews, the scholar is referred to as a *"talmid chacham."* The label, however, does not seem to make sense. Why use the word *talmid*, which means student? A student in a secular venue is one who has not yet completed a course of study. He is therefore not yet educated in the full sense. In the world of the yeshivah, however, the reverse is true. The greater a scholar becomes, the more of a *talmid chacham* he is — the more of a student he is. There is no such thing as completing the course of study. The Kotzker Rebbe, *zt"l*, explained it in this manner: a *chacham* can be a *chacham* only if he realizes that forever he must be a *talmid*. Our learning is never complete.

Another key term is the word *chinuch* itself. In numerous places Rashi points out that the verb *chanoch* means "an expression of beginning" (see *Devarim* 2:5 and *Rashi* there; see also *Devarim* 7:11 and Rashi's gloss in *Shevuos* 15a; et al.). As much *chinuch* as a person might receive, he will be considered a *mechanech* if and only if he considers himself to have only begun his learning. Ironically a *ben Torah* can never refer to himself as "educated" if the context is Torah. Even if he has become a *talmid chacham*, he is still only a student, is he not?

So how do we measure the success of *chinuch* when it reflects on an individual? It depends on how much the *melamed* has infused this idea of having to — being compelled to — always learn more. In simpler terms, if a child has gone through a class with a desire to learn more, then he is a *mechanech*. The teaching must be geared to this. A *melamed* must breed a love for learning — a *cheishek* — in order for him to be successful. Bestow on the child not merely the knowledge of *"Eilu Metzios"* or a quantity of *mishnayos* — bestow on him a burning desire to learn.

The same need not be true regarding GS. It can be, but this is not its stated goal.

Another source for illustration is this: In the Gemara (*Makkos* 8b) we find the declaration that when one is harsh with his son when trying to lead him to a deeper level of righteousness or Torah study, one is doing a mitzvah, even if the son is presently learning or conducting himself properly. If, on the other hand, one is overly harsh toward his son as part of an effort to direct him from a particular vocation to a better one, the father is *not* doing a mitzvah.

The ramifications for a pedagogic imperative are obvious.

THERE IS ANOTHER primary factor. What sort of perspective arises out of the learning process? My contention is that *chinuch* must provide a total perspective, while GS will provide only a limited one. And although secular educational philosophers have spoken of giving a student a "cognitive perspective," what they mean is that a child must receive training in a broad array of skills and disciplines rather than one or just a few. A cognitive perspective, though, is not a total perspective.

As an illustration, think about this: even those who would espouse a breadth of learning within the scope of GS would agree that there are certain areas of life that are taboo and cannot be discussed in the classroom. Imagine the flack a public school teacher might receive if he attempted to convince his young charges about a certain political view. In GS there must be limits. And this makes sense, because GS is not sacred; it is not learning undertaken for intrinsic value.

Chinuch is different, because the perspective has to

be total. Torah studies can broach the widest variety of issues from all facets of life. Racial matters, politics, war, death, personal morality, hygiene — it's all there in the limelight in the classroom of a rebbe or *morah*. There is virtually no area — religious, social, physical — that is left undiscussed in the Torah that can be taught. (Certainly there are restrictions as to what should be taught at which level, but that is not because of any limitations within the scope of the learning itself.)

As a result of this, a student of *limudei kodesh* should inherit from his teachers a total perspective, which ultimately is the ability to view all matters through the looking glass of *Yiddishkeit*. Matters will be decided by him based on their adherence to, or variance from, the teachings of Torah (and regarding those matters the student cannot decide on his own he will have learned to ask a *rav* or rebbe).

ANOTHER DISTINCTION between GS and *limudei kodesh*, really a byproduct of earlier distinctions, is the dimension of emulation. Does the teacher's role include being a role model for his students for ethical and other levels of behavior? Standards today are such that in the outside world the teacher need not necessarily be a prototype of desired behavior. It might be beneficial if the teacher were, but his being so is not an integral part of his role. There is no principle of emulation in the realm of non-Jewish education.

How might a teacher be emulated by his students? Children are liable to imitate speech patterns and dress modes, but there would be no cry of protest from parents, since these are of relatively little significance. But there are other things. If a teacher were discovered to be racist, to be verbally abusive, to be permissive, would he still be considered acceptable in the general world? Opinions do fluctuate, as might be seen from the incidence of this type of thing over the years, but as a rule parents would want that sort of person out of the classroom where he can do no harm to their children.

The reason for such parental reaction is that children are inclined to emulate. Parents would say these days that they do not *want* their children to emulate their teachers, but they fear that they might.

In *chinuch* the situation differs. The fundamental role of a rebbe, almost by definition, includes that he be a behavioral prototype. His job has sanctity, providing new links in the chain that reaches back to Sinai. His life must be lived in accordance with what he teaches. He cannot be what we might call a pareve personality, because in true *chinuch* there really is no such thing. A rebbe may not be a thief, for instance, for he teaches Torah, which states that a person may not be a thief. A *morah* may not desecrate Shabbos, for she teaches the laws of the Torah, which include that the Shabbos is holy.

And what about an English teacher in a yeshivah setting? As far as a child's need to have a teacher who is a role model, since the child in a yeshivah will have a rebbe or a *morah*, that need is satisfied (it is hoped!). The GS teacher does not have to be a role model, then, in the full sense of the word.

Second, since being a role model is not implicit in

the task of teaching GS, and since the only thing to fear is that children might emulate certain negative behaviors, then it should suffice that the GS teacher not be a negative force. He may be pareve, though. It would also be acceptable for him to be non-Jewish (there is little fear that a yeshivah student is going to emulate his non-Jewish GS teacher and go on to become nonobservant).

But if a GS teaching candidate is a good example of adherence to Torah, then he is preferable. Although being a role model is not vital to his task of teaching GS, it is advantageous for him to be one.

There is an additional reason for GS teachers to be *"heimishe"* people. It will elevate the profile of GS in the minds of students. Thus it will diminish the adversarial position many Torah students take to GS in the afternoon (more about that in the next chapter).

The Torah enjoins us, "And you shall cling to Him [the Almighty]" (*Devarim* 10:20). The Gemara asks (*Kesubos* 111b), is it possible to cling to the Creator? The well-known answer is cling to the scholars in order to learn from their ways. When the Mishnah tells us that we should "sit amid the dust of their feet" (*Avos* 1:4), referring to *talmidei chachamim*, it means learning from their ways and emulating them. The child who sits every day before a man whom he calls "rebbe" views him as someone from whom to learn the proprieties of life.

The Torah idealizes the notion of emulation, so the Torah teacher must be a suitable role model. The GS teacher does not have to be, but how fortunate are those students whose GS teachers are as much role models as the rebbes who teach them Torah!

Does Chol Belong in the Yeshivah?

A great many schools offer a dual curriculum — *kodesh* and *chol*. The main danger involved in this type of setup is that the two branches may generate two distinct — and often contradictory — sets of values. This presents students with an ongoing conflict, because ultimately the extent to which they lean toward one set of values will be equal to the extent to which they deny or lean away from the other. When it comes to sentiment, a child is a vessel, and just as a vessel cannot contain more than its capacity, a child cannot maintain two full measures of love for two distinct programs, especially when the child perceives conflict.

The confusion that results from a dual program is tantamount to unrest or psychological misery. However, that would not be the case if the two programs were of obviously different importance to the students. Thus a *chassidishe* or *yeshivish* school will not need to be concerned about its students having this conflict — it's *kodesh* over *chol* hands down. And the reverse might unfortunately be true in a very progressive Jewish school where the students have been raised with a first love for GS and Torah studies are at best a tolerated stepparent.

The difficulty will exist in a school where there is real balance (a virtue in most of life's areas) between *kodesh* and *chol*. In such a place, the operatives of education — the principals, the teachers — must teach that one set of values is primary and the other subordinate. A Torah school will therefore build up the Torah sentiment and make all else subordinate to it.

But the question is what are GS doing in a yeshivah at all? Not a simple question. One of the leading *gedolei hador* living in Eretz Yisrael declared a few years ago that it is forbidden to teach GS in a yeshivah and that this is destructive of the proper and holistic Torah atmosphere. An American *rav* opened a yeshivah in Eretz Yisrael where GS were taught, and this particular *gadol* banned attendance at the school. On the other hand, one of the leading *gedolei hador* living in the U.S. — in fact, one who has always followed strictly the guidance of the *gadol* in Israel — is famous for his tough position in support of GS. Boys in his yeshivah have said that they were told by him, after they had requested to be exempt from GS so that they could learn Torah the entire day, that they either take their GS seriously or they can look for another yeshivah.

THE PATTERN THAT seems to have emerged over the decades since the Second World War is that in Eretz Yisrael the more right-wing types of school, both *yeshivish* and *chassidish*, will not allow GS at the high-school level, and even at the elementary-school level GS is limited. Should it be that way? It is not our place to decide if *gedolim* have already decided the matter. One thing is obvious, though. In Eretz Yisrael it is far more possible for yeshivah children to survive without GS, because the language of society is the same as the one in which they are conducting much of their studies. So they require less formal training in other areas.

In Europe and America the trend, even among the most *frum* schools, is that GS is taught at least at the elementary level. I believe, however, that this merely reflects the fact that we are in the type of *galus* today that requires our being functionally literate, that we possess certain skills that allow us to get along reasonably and respectably in society.

This concept was once disputed by a gentleman under whose auspices I taught. He felt that when Rav Shamshon Raphael Hirsch, *zt"l*, spoke and wrote about the virtues of *"Torah im derech eretz"* he intended to say that this was the highest ideal of education in general and had nothing at all to do with the particular situation in which the Jewish people living in Germany found itself. I countered that there was no doubt in my mind that *Torah im derech eretz* was a policy developed and promoted by Rav Hirsch as a measure against assimilation among German Jews and the corrosiveness of *Yiddishkeit* that resulted from the Reform and Conservative movements.

Would Rav Hirsch have pushed the philosophy of *Torah im derech eretz* if he had been living in Poland or

Lithuania? My contention was that he would not have. Would he have suggested that the *chinuch* the children of Polish and Lithuanian Jews were receiving was deficient since it did not include GS? My contention was — and is — that he would not have made this suggestion.

I BELIEVE THAT the fact that yeshivos in the U.S. and Europe do offer GS today is not because they have adopted the policy of *Torah im derech eretz* as an ultimate ideal, but rather as a provisional one to help us deal with conditions. Still, the bottom line is that GS does occupy a spot in the Torah educational structure outside Eretz Yisrael today. (An Israeli *rosh yeshivah* once commented to me that in his opinion the elementary level of education there would stand to gain if it were to demand more GS there, too.)

So the question of whether GS belongs in the yeshivah is moot. Even if we accept that ideally it does not, it is still there, and we must deal with it. Properly.

A prominent *rosh yeshivah* from the Midwest, a recognized *gadol b'Yisrael*, said that if a student takes his GS less than seriously he transgresses the sin of *bitul Torah*. The reason is simple. If he is using time that ideally would be spent on Torah to his advantage, then the Torah permits it. If that time is wasted, however, then not only is the advantage not forthcoming, but wasted time is also *bitul Torah* by definition. This concept must be conveyed to the students.

A related notion is that *bitul zeman* is a terrible crime. With the precious little time we are allotted in this world it is our mission to accomplish that which we must accomplish. If we squander time, we are deficient. If GS time in the afternoon of a yeshivah's typical day is wasted and denigrated, then the child picks up and internalizes this terrible habit of *bitul zeman*, wasting time. This can have long-reaching effects on the way he will function in general, including the way he learns Torah. This concept must also be conveyed to students.

The classic axiom heard among parents of Torah students is something I agree with entirely. "If the children are learning English, at least let them do it properly."

Who Will Teach Our Children Chol?

In these trying times, one of the most challenging phenomena facing principals is recruiting able and efficient teachers for general studies. Parents want high standards of literacy and acumen in math, social sciences, and communicative skills. Well, the matter is not a simple one.

Based on all that we have said about GS there is little doubt about it: if someone is considering the choice between teaching Torah or teaching GS, there is no reason to opt for GS. Torah has value that is intrinsic; it is *chochmas Elokim*. GS lack these qualities (although there is certainly much in it that might also qualify as *chochmas Elokim*). Still, let us consider the question of whether GS could be at least a second choice or an additional undertaking.

ONE YEAR, AS I was lining up my staff for the upcoming academic season, I was faced with a challenging task —

hiring a good math and science teacher for the seventh grade. The classes that were moving up to seventh grade were...well, let's just say they, too, were challenging. I knew I needed someone good. As noted earlier, my personal policy has always been to try to hire rebbes for GS, assuming they are amenable, available, and qualified. I wished that such a possibility would arise for the seventh grade.

Then it struck me. In the yeshivah where I was principal, there was a *melamed* in one of the primary grades whom I knew would be perfect for the job. And I knew that not long ago he had purchased a house and that he would be strapped for funds. If there were an additional source of income, he might at least consider it. At the same time I knew my offer would be pitted against layers of hangups (I'm afraid this is the best expression for it!) over getting involved in teaching GS. And I was quite familiar with those hangups, since I had entertained them myself at one point in my life no less than anyone else with a yeshivah background.

Fortunately I decided to take the chance of offering him the position, complete with a lecture on the importance of having *heimishe* GS teachers and announcing what the bottom line would be in dollars and cents.

The initial response was much as I had predicted. Though enticed by the monetary benefit, he was uncomfortable with the idea and said he was being *"noteh"* to turning me down. "But let me discuss it at home," he said, adding that he would give me a clearer picture the following day.

I did not hold forth a great deal of hope, because I

understood what it meant for a *ben Torah*, a rebbe in a yeshivah, to suddenly appear before the world with a new persona, a new visage — that of an "English teacher." Something told me, however, that his wife might shed a different light on the issue for him. Women, who are often concerned with the finances of the home, often have a better appreciation for a bottom line than their more idealistic husbands do. So I figured the rebbe would have a shmooze at home, and his wife might persuade him that being a GS teacher is not so terrible, especially in light of the fact that he would not be giving up his main career and image of being a rebbe and doing *meleches Hashem*.

I could not have been more wrong. He came into my office the next day with the distressing news (at least, I thought it was distressing) that his wife did not like the idea at all. "You're a rebbe," she had told him. "You didn't go into *chinuch* to become an English teacher." Actually, I was impressed. My thoughts turned to the wife of On ben Peles who saved her errant husband from the doom he'd have met had he continued to be part of the conspiracy of Korach.

Then my heart changed on the matter. I might even say that I was a bit insulted. Could one not be both a rebbe and an English teacher (or principal)? After all, I was. Additionally I felt that the expression "English teacher" was voiced with disdain, as if it were *nivul peh*. I was very good at concealing my objection to the thought that underlay his answer, though I was very open in showing my disappointment.

ALL IN ALL, I wasn't ready to throw in the towel just yet. I had a trick up my sleeve, although I should not even refer to it as a trick. I knew that on the very next day one of the most renowned *roshei yeshivah* of contemporary times, a *gadol b'Yisrael*, was due to arrive in Toronto for a visit. I also knew that the rebbe whom I was trying so desperately to convince to join my GS staff was a *talmid* of that *rosh yeshivah* and maintained an extremely close relationship with him though years had gone by since he had left the yeshivah. I had an idea. "One minute. Rav X. is coming to town tomorrow, right? You're going to see him, right? Why don't you just ask him his opinion about this idea of mine?"

"You know what? Maybe I will," he responded, evidently confident that his *rosh yeshivah* would agree with the decision that he had made, or should I say, that his wife had made with him. I, on the other hand, was not quite as certain of this.

The next afternoon he came back into my office and told me the news. The *rosh yeshivah* did not even seem to understand why the question needed to be asked. Of course he could teach GS in the yeshivah. What could possibly be wrong with it?

So he asked me once again the details of the financial agreement and accepted my offer of a job. That was nearly a decade ago. He has never looked back since. Today he is still a rebbe and still a seventh-grade math and science teacher. I do not believe that he has even the slightest regret over his decision (apart from some afternoons that might tax his endurance!). And I know for certain that over the years he has taught a few hundred yeshivah children skills they learned much better and more easily because it was he who had taught it to them. And I know that there are hundreds of people who appreciate greatly the opportunity to have learned some GS at the hands of this rebbe.

And I know that when people conjure up the image of that particular person they conjure up the image of a rebbe in a yeshivah who also teaches some GS, rather than that of a GS teacher who also teaches *kodesh*. His primary role is *meleches Hashem*, and his long ago choice to also enter the GS field did not detract, at least as far as I can see, from his persona. In fact, in the eyes of most, it enhanced it.

So if I were the one being asked by a young prospective *mechanech* about whether *chol* should be among his prospects, I would be honest with him. I would tell him that in a *frum* school the GS part of the day is the most difficult in many respects. But the more *bnei Torah* who teach GS, the higher the overall profile *chol* will have among the boys. If the profile will one day be sufficiently high, then we can expect a higher yield as well as an easier time producing it.

I will emphasize once again, though, that with all my urging, one proviso must always be borne in mind: qualifications or, more correctly stated, ability. Do not enter this or any field unless you possess the skills that are necessary for you to succeed. As an employer of teachers, I have also had experiences somewhat different from the one described above. I once hired a professional with the assumption that he would succeed at teaching GS. I was wrong. Training, a bit of secular education, and a lot of common sense — these are the prerequisites a *melamed* must have in order to become a GS teacher.

In Chazal we often find the expression *"chullin al taharas hakodesh,"* which fundamentally refers to the strictness with which holy people, such as *kohanim*, would eat, or prepare, plain food. As a sign of their piety, they treated the mundane as if it were sacred. The *chullin* did not actually get transformed into *kodesh* via the stringency of the *kohanim*; it was merely treated as such, since that treatment was the natural extension of their piety.

Similarly, there will always be a distinction between the way we want our children to view *chol* and the way they deal with *kodesh*. However, it is important for us as parents as well as *mechanchim* to impart this notion of *"chullin al taharas hakodesh"* — that true piety necessitates that we do virtually everything in a sacred manner, just like the *kohanim* of long ago.

Part Six

SPECIAL STUDENTS

Introduction

Every *mechanech* has special students. Except for a purely elitist situation, which may have ethical problems of its own, every school and every class have students with special needs. The past two decades have seen these students move into the center stage of *chinuch*. Many teachers in training choose to enter the specialized field of special education, and many a seminar at many a convention have been devoted to the highly complex topic, teaching parents coping strategies and teachers professional techniques.

What is so important is that things have changed drastically concerning special students. The Gemara (*Baba Basra* 22b) discusses what ought to be done with the child who is unable to keep up with his classmates. The determination of Chazal is that *"lehevei tzavsa l'chavrei,"* that he should remain with his group of peers. This means it is not permitted to ostracize him or to exclude him from learning. Whatever he picks up he picks up.

If the Gemara needed to enunciate this position, it is

obvious that there was an opinion that held that special students may be excluded. That should come as no surprise, because it was common for a child who had difficulties to be expelled from his class or even the school. It was therefore important for the Gemara to clarify that this is forbidden.

One situation I can recall shows how far people may go to further the case for removing special students from the regular group. A boy was having varied difficulties in yeshivah, so his parents, acting with alarm, decided to take him for analysis by one of the city's "top" children's learning psychologists. After a costly series of visits and an exhaustive battery of tests, the professional concluded that it was unhealthy for the boy to be in a program that expected him to carry a dual load, that is, a *kodesh* curriculum in addition to that of *chol*. His suggestion — it cannot be graced with the accolade of prescription — was that the boy be withdrawn from yeshivah and sent to a regular public school.

We know that keeping *all* Jewish children in a yeshivah is paramount, and I need not belabor this point. At the same time, the purpose of having the special student remain within a classroom, if indeed that is what will be done, is twofold. First, he will be able to do some measure of learning, according to his level, of course. Second, he will not be made to feel as if he does not belong. What needs to be considered, though, is what are the best methods of achieving these two goals.

In my mind there is little question that to some extent the two goals might be mutually exclusive. The reason, in a nutshell, is this: serving the special student's specialized needs best, from an academic standpoint, would require placing him in a resource room, perhaps even in a resource facility, that is, an entirely independent school or setting. Today, in major Jewish communities around the world, there exist such schools or programs, which have met with varying degrees of success.

Alternatively, it has been argued, usually with emotion, that putting a child into such a venue, where he is isolated and comes to view himself as second class or inferior, will do such devastating damage to his self-concept that he can possibly be emotionally maimed for the rest of his life.

Some of those who have espoused that argument rally behind the flag of integration, which calls on schools to integrate special students — even those who are severely challenged — within the larger learning frameworks. Ethically this seems to conform with the words of the Gemara. There are two hefty price tags, however, which should not be forgotten.

First, full integration will in all likelihood not promote the academic advancement of the special student as much as a resource room. It cannot. Second is the ramifications for the teacher. Much more must be expected of him, because he must address at least two (and possibly many more than two) levels of study. He must train; he must develop special patience. Most teachers lack the necessary personality and know-how to deal with the challenge with aplomb.

There are also ramifications for the classmates of integrated, special-needs children. On the negative side, the teacher might be compelled to devote an inordinately high portion of his time to the special child, and there might be less learning going on as a result. Boredom could set in and possibly resentment. On the positive side is the benefit these classmates will enjoy in terms of their social skills. They will have matured through the experience, and they will have learned the all-important virtues of tolerance and helping others who need it.

It is a complex issue to sift through. The situation that is perhaps the best, because it satisfies more of the needs of the special student, is when a combined program is offered, in which he could have some resource-room time to assist him, but most of his time will be spent in the classroom. Obviously the formula will vary with the individual.

Meanwhile, as the battle rages on between the supporters of integration (sometimes it goes by the name of "inclusion") and between the supporters of the resource-room concept, the teacher faces a situation in which a portion of his or her student body will have special needs, at least of a moderate nature. My experience has shown that on the average there are between fifteen and twenty percent of the population of an average class that presents special learning needs. The educator is therefore going to be expected to deal with that fact. He might have the good fortune of being provided some assistance by his administration or he might not. In the final analysis, however, responsibility might fall squarely into his lap.

What about the parents? They, of course, want what's best for their child. There are, however, emotional

Introduction

issues, such as denial, which may cloud a parent's thinking on a specific matter. Since a parent often views his child as an extension of himself, a parent's acceptance of a shortcoming in a child is equivalent to acceptance of that shortcoming in himself.

It is best if the parent tries to divorce his own self-concept from the profile of the child. The teacher's summation of a situation and the guidance of other *mechanchim* (and possibly of mental-health professionals) will ultimately benefit the child the most. That is what is best for him.

At the same time, it should be understood that though a teacher cannot become a special-education expert overnight (or possibly ever), he or she has no moral right to ignore special-needs children or to avoid dealing with them. Read on, then, as I outline for you a number of vital ideas to help you sail the troubled waters of dealing with special-needs children.

Labels

Today's *melamed* and *morah* are in danger of giving in to a new sort of pedagogic temptation — labeling. Mental-health experts who deal with the learning problems children face have offered to educators over the years a handsome array of resource-room labels, which makes the pedagogue sound so professional by merely mentioning them. School staff rooms and principals' offices have been inundated with the reverberations of such terms as dyslexia, hyperactivity, attention-deficit disorder (ADD), decoding block, weak retentive skills, fine- and gross-motor coordination weakness and on and on. Some parents, forever seeking to be abreast of the latest educational advances, also make use of such labels in their own analyses.

The reason I suggest that the use of these labels is a temptation particularly for today's teachers is not because I suppose that what they really want is to sound professional. I have a much higher opinion of *melamdim* than that. The reason that it is a temptation is that ever since these brands have been bandied about by every educational expert wannabe, teachers are prone to cite them as magical exemptions from taking responsibility. Teachers will thus say things like, "How can I possibly get through to Yanky? After all, he has ADD." Or, "I am not about to repeat things endlessly for the benefit of Yossi. I can't help it if he has dyslexia." Or, "Shaindy? Forget about her. She is LD (learning disabled)."

In large measure, before the labels were invented, teachers who faced difficulty with a particular student would either take the bull by the horns and work harder for the benefit of the child or he would not. But he never considered the notion that he was exempt from the task. Today even outstanding educators tend to consign the special student to the realm of nonachievement because the labels have categorized him as a child who belongs there.

Alternatively, diagnosing certain symptoms as being caused by specific deficiencies in the child may be helpful in reaching out to that child. In the same way that a physician knows that not all fevers are symptomatic of the same illness, and that each situation must be treated in its own distinct fashion, the parent and the teacher need to be as diagnostic as they can be so that those children who are specially challenged can be treated in the appropriate fashion. Ultimately this is what was meant by Shlomo HaMelech's classical charge to *mechanchim*, "*Chanoch lana'ar al pi darko* — Train each child in his own way" (*Mishlei* 22:16).

What is more important than that, however, is that being diagnostic will allow a teacher to maintain a stance that is so fundamental — the stance of compassion.

FOR THE LONGEST time it was assumed that a child who is not learning simply refuses to. It was assumed, perhaps, that all children have more or less the same capacity to learn (although it was always recognized that certain children were geniuses and others were extremely underendowed). So if a child was not learning, what other conclusion could be drawn but that "he is rebellious," "he refuses to learn," "he is *chutzpahdik*," "he enjoys daydreaming"?

Now I do agree that sometimes it is true that the child just won't learn even though he is perfectly capable. But usually there is a reason. A child may be rebellious, but there is a legitimate explanation for that. A child may be daydreaming, but it is possible that the teacher is boring him to bits. All learning tendencies can be reduced to specific causes. More often than not, the causes are related to the student. But sometimes it is connected to the teacher, the peer group, or a myriad of other factors.

Once upon a time parents would immediately get upset with a child who brought home a failing grade. Fortunately, today many parents are astute enough to realize that there is likely a reasonable explanation for the grade. In some cases, parents are inspecting their own parenting techniques in search of a possible deficiency there. Some parents discover that they are not devoting enough time to their children, while others find that they tend to anger far too easily while attacking school studies with their children. This attempt at introspection can only be helpful to the child.

A teacher is morally bound to try to unearth what is troubling the child. Once, years ago, when a teacher who worked for me noted that one of her students always shied away from active participation in any of the oral activities of the class and as a result was dropping in his overall output, she wondered whether or not there might not be an auditory problem. When she probed and recommended to the family that a hearing test be done, they determined that, sure enough, there was a medical — and, *baruch Hashem*, easily treatable — reason that the boy was not hearing properly. Within a few short weeks, the problem had been solved, and the boy was on the road to higher grades and a stronger self-image.

Certainly not all stories are as elementary as that one, but the account suffices to illustrate that if the adults in a child's world will be alert to aberrations and compassionate enough to stop and consider what might be the cause of them — other than saying that the child is "negative" — then many of the challenges of special students can be dealt with successfully. Begin with the assumption that a child would not be negative without a just explanation — it is a sound assumption.

ANOTHER OF THE most common sources of so-called negativity on the part of a child has nothing to do with either the teacher or with any learning disability. It too has merited its very own label: family dysfunction. Sadly the contemporary world is one in which expressions such as "divorced," "separated," "broken home," and "custody battle" are all too common. Children suffer in untold ways from these trends.

Then there is an assortment of abuses administered by some parents — physical, verbal, emotional, and otherwise. Often the telltale signs that something is amiss are not clearly visible. A teacher must bear in mind, though, that these scenarios are prevalent in contemporary society, and they are at the source of many of the problems children face. The teacher should be prepared to help fill an emotional gap in his student, although this might be fraught with a host of difficulties.

Being a crusader and attempting to rectify the wrongs that affect a child's world may lie beyond the scope of the teacher's responsibility. Some teachers want to rise to the task and pry into matters that are not remotely part of their jurisdiction. It is hoped that a responsible *mechanech* will use common sense before attacking the larger situation. The best thing a teacher can do is to understand what the student might be going through and unobtrusively manipulate his or her situation so that the child will suffer less.

Truth be told, there are far too many variables related to this topic to be discussed here with academic integrity. I do not entertain the hope that this meager chapter serves as an exhaustive resource. If anything, I seek to inculcate into the heart and the mind of the parents and the educators the idea that there is no child who has an inexplicable negativity toward school or learning. There is no child who is afflicted with a bad personality or a troubled predisposition.

All challenges are derived from something. Try to found out what it is. Do not throw labels around. Employ whatever sensitivity and common sense you can muster to help defuse the crisis your child might be going through.

Above all, understand him, tolerate him, help him. You might be saving him in the process.

Part Seven

VARIED VIEWPOINTS

Introduction

We have come almost full circle. We mentioned much earlier the "problem of other minds," the communication barrier that exists between those who are *mechanchim* and those who are not. Additionally, the barrier is never as poignantly felt as in the relationship between a *melamed* and the parents of the students he teaches. So essential is the maintenance of a positive state of mind on the part of the educators and parents, one in which they stretch their perceptions in order to comprehend what the other sees and feels, that, as I pointed out, a separate chapter on this theme is warranted.

Undoubtedly there would be a meaningful advantage to addressing parents alone on the same theme, but this is not the venue for that. Here we are concentrating mainly on the point of view of the *mechanech*.

Besides, teachers for the most part are parents, too. They are the ones who are in a better position to comprehend both sides of the divide. In fact, as educators who are parents, they often find themselves in a position of conflict. I have even seen them act toward the teachers of their own children in the exact same manner that they would take exception to if they were on the receiving end. (Nothing like a bit of subjectivity to alter an approach!) Perhaps this is why Hillel gave the world the golden rule, "Do not do to others what you would not want others to do to you" (*Shabbos* 31a).

The Great Divide

In the Haggadah we read Chazal's explanation of the words *"v'es amaleinu* — and our toil," the toil of the Jews of Egypt. *"Eilu habanim,"* explain our Sages, refers to children. We live for our children. The Jew invests the lion's share of his strengths and resources in his children. They are the most precious things in our lives. When the parent consigns his child into the hands of a teacher, he is entrusting to him what is most precious to him in the entire world. A teacher must never lose sight of that, because essentially that is what lies at the base of the outlook parents have toward a school and its functionaries.

I would therefore contend that difficulties might arise in the relationship between parent and teacher when there is suspicion that the teacher is taking the mission too lightly. A *melamed* needs to remember that he is a *shaliach* for the parent.

Conversely, many, if not most, of the features of a child's performance in school are not the making of teachers, but rather the function of parenting. Still, a teacher cannot suggest to a parent that in his opinion the parent is taking his or her job as parent too lightly. If anything will aggravate the communication, that surely will, although the hypothesis is very often correct, at least as often as the contention that a teacher is deficient. As a rule, of course, it is essential to avoid any mudslinging, not to mention ethical.

To be sure, when a child learns well and is content, there is little concern that there will be barriers to communication between *melamed* and parent. But nothing is as effective as a bit of failure or discontent to throw contention into the equation. This, then, becomes the medium of fathoming the workings of the teacher-parent schism: failure.

Through the Cracks

At a wedding a number of years ago, I sat with a number of *rabbanim* during the *seudas mitzvah*. The conversation took a turn to the topic of *chinuch*, and in particular to the issue of Jewish youth who are, to use the popular expression, "falling through the cracks."

One prominent local Torah personality seated next to me whispered to me that he could easily furnish for me a list of thirty cases here in town whose aberrant behavior was already edging dangerously close to the "big three *aveiros*" (that is, those which one must desist from committing even at the cost of his life — "*yeihareig v'al ya'avor*"). Thirty in New York would be only mildly disconcerting, but in a secondary level community such as Toronto, that figure is alarming, especially in light of the fact that in the few years that have elapsed the number has increased dramatically.

The real shock, of course, was when he told me that most of these were youths from fine Torah homes.

In my horror I began to ponder the believability of

his claim, and I found that a number of cases did come to mind. When I thought more about it, it became frighteningly clear that compiling such a list would probably not be too difficult and that the number could very well exceed what he had said.

These young people are the *aseres hashevatim* of Jewish education; they are becoming the "lost children." When we consider what has happened to them, we find various landscapes. One may have left the ramparts of Torah altogether without any other apparent aberrations, while another, when eyes are not upon him, heads to some dark netherworld to pursue his pleasures. Another may be denying the centrality of Torah in his life and as a result lives quite apart from it, while still another may have slid into the shadows of crime and substance abuse. What they seem to have in common is a sense of cynicism. Some have even become nihilistic, whereby their lives appear to be devoted to nothing in particular. No goal is important enough, and no plan is undertaken.

Some cases are more severe, while some are mild (an adjective used too easily, I am sure, by an untouched third party). However, they all share a common thread: they are enactments of a rebellion of sorts. These youths are in reality proclaiming, via their lifestyle choices, "The system has failed me. Now I am going to fail *it* — in a big way!"

What's going on?

Although I have no statistical information available, no facts and figures of dropout rates — in fact, I do not believe that any such data exists altogether — I would dare suggest that the phenomenon is not new. Jewish youth falling through the cracks is a syndrome that has always existed. What may be new, however, is the recent openness and frankness regarding the problem. Consequently there is perhaps more hope of dealing with the trend than there used to be in the old days.

Denial used to be the order of the day. Parents and educators alike would deny the portent or the very existence of early symptoms, until it was too late — some young person had already taken the plunge. And once that plunge had been taken, well, it was deemed irrevocable. Nobody wanted to discuss the issue or even mention the name of the "perpetrator."

I recall hearing many years ago one local administrator saying, "Such cases do not exist in our school." Well, they sure did, and they do today. In that school and in every school. And it is not derisive for today's *mosdos* to recognize this reality and the need to deal with it. And it is not shameful for a community at large to face the fact that these situations are everywhere in our midst, and as a community it behooves us to address them. The adults who play roles in the lives of children are compelled to address them.

WHAT ARE THE causes of the trend? One of the major causes is the plethora of challenges children may face in their schooling years. These range from attention deficit disorder (ADD) and hyperactivity to dyslexia, reasoning, and processing blocks and a variety of other learning disabilities. Although *mechanchim* should not make excessive use of labels, the deficiencies do exist and may be dealt with objectively.

Some challenges are social, some academic, while others might be emotional. A child afflicted with such a challenge may find that he or she does not fit into the social framework. Perhaps he learns more slowly, perhaps he retains little, maybe he cannot sit long enough to concentrate, and he accomplishes little of a positive nature. So he compensates by accomplishing things of a negative nature, and he gets into lots of trouble with his teachers. The problems can become severely aggravated with time. It begins with a young child conceiving of himself as a "real case." One thing leads to the next, and by the time he is an adolescent or older, he has lost all conscious desire of making it in the traditional setting, and he has in reality become a case.

Schools can and should do what they can to avoid the development of the problems and to treat them when they have germinated. Success may be limited, but the efforts are a must. Yet the school is by no means the only breeding ground for the difficulty. Many of the youths who stray are good learners and very much adjusted in their academic lives.

One source of the problem could be incompetence on the part of a teacher. I have found that nearly every adult has an easy time thinking back to at least one teacher whom he had in school who completely "turned him off." While in some cases the teacher may have been blameless, at times the problem may have boiled down to a teacher who lacked either the skill or the sensitivity needed to deal with a situation properly. In some instances, the damage done by a teacher may have been so profound that the child subjected to his or her abuses might have become intensely negative to all teachers, all schools, all learning, and much of what is commonly held to be social propriety. So a teacher who shouts, insults, humiliates, or uses corporal punishment abusively may be unwittingly creating a dysfunctional individual.

Another common source is the dysfunctional family. There may be a lack of *shalom bayis* or an abusive parent. In another home the financial stress may be so great that the child may not be being fed adequately. And how many adults are so busy with their careers, their businesses, or their leisure lives that they have too little time for their children? A very common related problem is that there is not a sufficient amount of love being generated within the family, and the child becomes insecure and suspicious.

The possibilities are numerous and terribly debilitating for a young person. They leave him ill equipped for healthy and productive interpersonal relationships. Thus he has difficulty with his classmates, with his rebbe and his teacher. These people, and authority figures in general, become symbols of all that makes this young person miserable and sad. And as he develops into an adult, he exhibits behavior patterns that vent this attitude. Before anyone has noticed, he has fallen through the cracks.

ONCE ONE HAS analyzed the causes of the problem, one has to deal with it. A good starting point is the realization that a child who falls through the cracks did not make a level-headed, intelligent, willful decision to do so. Somewhere along the line he fell victim to circumstances. If we incorrectly view the scenarios as *mezidim*, intentional evildoing, then we only alienate these victims. If we understand that their condition is a manifestation of something that was not right for them, and something which in all likelihood was beyond their control, then we develop the all-important fundamental empathy that will promote our ability to reach out and help.

At a recent national convention of the Agudath Israel of America, one of the sessions featured a symposium of two experts, who are involved, albeit in different ways, in dealing with such youths. As they related some of the cases they confronted, I detected muffled cries here and there from different places in the overflow crowd. As real-life situations were described in detail, the audience sat spellbound. We all seemed to recognize the circumstances; the depictions were close to home. The story of a *bachur* who was not successful in yeshivah and left to seek greener pastures was all too familiar. So was that of a young girl who decided that *frumkeit* was not for her and stopped keeping Shabbos.

The upshot, however, was rather upbeat. Things were being done. Schools are now more alert to the problem areas that lie within their domain. For older youths, drop-in centers are being opened where young Jews who are having difficulty can come and spend some time in a welcoming and noncritical environment. Competent people are being engaged to attempt this highly sensitive and specialized type of outreach. Things are happening!

Still, as responsible parents and *mechanchim*, it is our divine duty to make every effort to ensure that the symptoms are dealt with early on. Needless to say, it is wiser to prevent the problem than to have to deal with it in its enhanced state later on.

In terms of dissecting the disparity of attitudes, I offer a pair of articles that were featured in *Perspectives* (published by Toronto's Agudah). Actually, they were abridged versions of articles that appeared in *Country Yossi Magazine*.* They poignantly outline the attitude of a yeshivah as opposed to the attitude of a parent in dealing with a difficult situation.

---

* Reprinted with permission from *Country Yossi Magazine*.

Cross-fire 2

This story is authentic, though the names and some of the details have been changed to protect the privacy of the individuals. The author, who prefers to remain anonymous for obvious reasons, knows the family well and shares their pain. Please print this letter, for the sake of the unfortunate bachur and others like him. If even one more boy is kept in a yeshivah another zeman because of it, it will have been worthwhile.

A Rejected Yeshivah Bachur

You may not recognize my handwriting, but my name is very familiar to you. I am the *bachur* you didn't accept back into your yeshivah this fall.

I know you're probably wondering what makes me write to you. After all, you told my parents that your decision was final. Actually, I'm not so sure of the reason myself; I guess part of it may be that I'm finding myself with too much time on my hands. As of now, five weeks into the *zeman*, I still haven't found a yeshivah that will accept me. After all, if you won't take back your own garbage, so to speak, why would anyone else?

Besides, I probably wouldn't have made it there either. If after five years of trying I wasn't deemed worthy enough of being allowed to continue learning within the hallowed halls of your yeshivah, I certainly will not be capable of success anywhere else.

Sorry. Don't mind my stinging sarcasm. It isn't me, only a coverup for the deep, intense pain I feel inside. It hasn't gone away since last Wednesday, when I overheard my father speaking to you and saw him wipe away his tears. That wasn't the first time I heard my father crying, but now I felt guilty because I was the cause. Anyhow, I secretly listened on the other line and heard you telling him plainly that I was a bad influence on the other boys and even had the nerve to speak during davening and joke around during learning time. Since you want to spare the other *bachurim* from my influence, you have no choice and cannot accept me back to the yeshivah this *zeman*. You sounded truly sorry, of course, but you felt that it was something you had to do.

In my family the phone conversation was the beginning of a night I'd rather not think about. The whipping and tongue-lashing I received was not nearly as painful as the familiar sight of my father crying, my mother moaning in hysteria, and the way they kept reminding me that nobody needed me and I was an utter, complete failure.

I knew that already. I'm of no use to you and very

little use to my family, and no *rosh yeshivah* in the area wants to take me in. If it wasn't so tragic, it would be almost funny. Because, discounting my troubled family background and my nonexistent self-esteem, I happen to be a pretty average *bachur*.

Sure, I spoke during davening once or twice and clowned around sometimes during learning. I always spread the latest news, and I'm usually one of the kids hanging around the coffee machine. But so is B., the son of a respected rabbi.

And take M., another one of the guys who can't wait to leave yeshivah and go into business. He's always the first one to look for trouble and often answers back instead of listening respectfully to his elders. The only difference is his father just paid for the renovations to the dormitory wing.

These boys are also fairly average, not the cream of the crop, and definitely not from the "learners," but are they branded as failures?

Is it a yeshivah for boys or a yeshivah for parents? Why should I suffer for my father's chronic heart problems and my mother's neurotic obsession with how miserable her life is? Did I choose the family I was born into? Why am I branded a failure when other boys who are no better or worse than I have glowing futures ahead of them? They'll marry the best girls, receive the best jobs, and have the most friends, while a specter of doom and failure surrounds me. Nobody needs me; I'm a yeshivah-less bum who sits home and argues with his parents or walks around the block looking for action. I'm the boy who "fell through the cracks" and is slowly headed for a life on the streets.

And here's the final question: are you willing to take responsibility for another lost *neshamah*? Is the price of tolerating my presence in your yeshivah, my possible distraction to the other boys (which is nonexistent; nobody needs me for a friend), another non-tuition-paying mouth to feed and bed in the yeshivah, too much to save my future?

What about *hatzalas nefashos*? Why does your heart bleed at the plight of Russian and Iranian boys (I saw you giving a handsome donation last *zeman*) and when it comes to a child within your community, it's none of your concern? "*Kol Yisrael areivim zeh lazeh.*" We're all part of one body, and you can no sooner write me off as you can say goodbye to your leg.

Let's face it: I'm not going to another yeshivah. I've been through it all — the meetings, interviews where I was subjected to intense scrutiny followed by the polite refusals. "I'm sorry. There are no more beds available." (What nonsense — I'll sleep on the floor.) "I'm sorry, we're all full." (The interview took place near the study hall, which was only three-quarters full.)

With each interview my father's blood pressure goes up a little more, and my mother hurls more insults. I've become like the floor — cold and hard — and I don't care anymore. It's my body's way of shutting out the pain.

I hope you haven't ripped up this letter by now. Just in case it hasn't done its job, I'm enclosing a picture of a hippie. In five years this may be me.

And while I have to take full responsibility for my actions, to a large extent you will be held culpable for letting me fall through the cracks. I stand now at the cross-roads. Won't you help me choose life? If not for my own sake, then for the sake of all my future generations?

Sincerely,
A rejected *yeshivah bachur*

A Menahel Replies to a Rejected Yeshivah Bachur

I read your letter and felt your deep pain and anguish. If only you could know the pain that I and my colleagues, your rebbes, felt when we made the agonizing decision that you could not remain in the yeshivah!

How I wish that you had shed just one little tear in all the times you were in my office. Then perhaps things would have been different.

For years the rebbes of the yeshiva were doing everything in their power to help you, but you resisted their every effort. They tolerated your outbursts of sarcasm, mockery, and arrogance, despite the great inner pain and embarrassment you caused them. They tried desperately to change your attitude, but you ignored them. You were obstinate, arrogant, and fearless, but they kept trying anyway. They tried to make you understand the serious consequences of your actions, but you only scoffed and ridiculed them behind their backs and even to their faces. Even then they were patient in the hope that the glow of Torah and their own concern for your welfare would gradually have an effect — but then you became a very negative influence to the other students who began to look up to you as a role model.

Yes, others began to imitate your ways! If only you would have felt the deep anguish in my heart when I pleaded with you lovingly to change your ways. Then perhaps your stone heart would have softened a bit.

Had you merely refused to learn, but not been a negative influence on other students, the yeshivah would have allowed you to stay. However, the question now was one of losing just one very precious soul or, *chas v'shalom*, losing many more.

Little do you know that on the day I had to make that fateful decision, I fasted all day. This was followed by many tearful and sleepless nights. Are we permitted to jeopardize the welfare of many of other *talmidim* in the hope that your negative influence would not harm them? The decision was made finally that we had no right to jeopardize other children. "*Mutav sheyechallel Shabbos achas v'al yechallel Shabbasos harbeh* — Better to desecrate one Shabbos than to desecrate many more." So we had to remove one student — you — rather than risk harm to many others.

It was a heartrending, difficult, and painful decision. I felt as Avraham Avinu must have felt on the day he had to ask his son Yishmael to leave his house. Despite Avraham's great love for his son, Hashem told him to follow Sarah's advice. Unfortunately we do not have a *navi* whom we can consult when making such a life-and-death decision. But we do have a *Shulchan Aruch*, which gives us the guidelines to follow. The halachah is clear. A child who does not learn but does not corrupt others should be allowed to remain in the classroom, but one who is disruptive and a negative influence on others must be asked to leave.

While you suggest that the yeshivah has shown a bias toward others with similar problems (because of their parents' wealth and other reasons), I assure you that this was not the case. Think back. There were other *talmidim* who left the yeshivah, including some of the famous and wealthy. You and your friends thought they had gone because they were dissatisfied with us and felt they would do better elsewhere. Often that was true. But there were other cases where we told their parents privately that we could no longer keep them — just as we spoke to your parents privately and with compassion.

You complain that we tolerated misbehavior on the part of others. True. But don't you remember how long we bent over backward for your sake as well? Believe me, if your parents had been major contributors, we would still have been obligated to put the benefit of so many others ahead of your insistence on doing everything you please. The "they did it, too" defense is a common rationalization for those who refuse to correct their own faults. It is only now that you have seen your parents' deep hurt and pain and that you are unable to be accepted into any other school that you are beginning to realize the damage you have caused yourself. But even now you are lashing out and blaming others instead of looking inward.

Yet all is not lost. As Rabbeinu HaKadosh cried and said, "*Yeish koneh olamo b'sha'ah achas* — One can acquire the World to Come in just one moment" — if one tries hard enough.

You can still change your ways if you really care to. It will take great will power and inner strength. I am always ready to help you in the privacy of my home, as long as it is not at the expense of others. And perhaps — I pray — we can take you back, if you show the desire to become a new person. Just remember, my dear child: the doors of *teshuvah* are never closed!

THE ISSUES ARE complex and highly charged with emotion. It is not my claim that the *she'eilah* should be answered here. Should the *bachur* have been expelled from the yeshivah or not? Let us abstain on that one, with the humble suggestion that *da'as Torah* must always be consulted before a drastic move is made. The fundamental point, however, is that the educator is not morally permitted to ever lose sight of the intensity of parental feeling that is involved in issues pertaining to his so-called difficult students.

A selfish reason that can motivate the teacher to keep his heart open is that by so doing he will generate a mutuality of warmth that can only benefit the teacher in the long and the short run. *Melamdim* tend to complain that parents are insensitive to them, while I have seen that the reverse is just as true. The cyclical movement can be halted; the educator might as well be the one to do it.

Postscript

Many stones have been left unturned in this work. The logistics and the how to's are largely left unaddressed. But the seas of *chinuch* are immense and deep; each and every Jewish child constitutes a new chapter unto himself.

My goal has not been to cover all eventualities and to provide a list of recipes. It has been merely to discuss some of the areas of Jewish education that hardly get discussed — some of the *hashkafah*, the history, the challenges...and the lighter side.

It has also been to open the vistas of communication whereby parents and educators might be better equipped to glimpse the cares and concerns that the other might have.

A person who has chosen *chinuch* as his life's work will need to have a reservoir of laughter and tolerance inside himself — and to draw from that reservoir often — if he is to survive and maintain a positive attitude.

A layman — and in particular a parent — will need to open his heart to the issues with which *mechanchim* grapple. The sensitivity to the challenges will ultimately result in strengthening teachers rather than alienating and disenfranchising them — helping them to shine rather than to falter.

What should always be remembered by *mechanchim*, though, is that the joys of teaching are the greatest joys and the most exhilarating highs that can be experienced. And, as is to be expected, something as grand as that cannot be offered to man without a price tag of trials and tribulations.